EXTRAORDINARY WARNINGS . . . AMAZING RESCUES
GUIDANCE IN LOVE AND TIMES OF TROUBLE.
READ THE AMAZING TRUTH ABOUT . . .

- The young man who was almost crushed under a station wagon until a powerful presence helped his companions lift the car to free him.
- The mother who is directed by an unseen voice—and slaps on her shoulder—in how to save her baby's life.
- The courageous police officer whose guardian angel saves her from drowning.
- The disembodied helping hand captured on film clearly enough for a spiritualist to read its palm.
- The singer who loses his voice on stage only to have his dead voice teacher complete the performance for him.
- The young father who dies in a tragic accident but returns a year later to protect his wife and child from harm.

—and scores of other inspirational true stories in

GUARDIAN ANGELS AND SPIRIT GUIDES

Brad Steiger is the author and co-author with his wife Sherry Hansen Steiger of more than 100 books with over 15 million copies in print, including *Amazing Moms* and *One With The Light* (both Signet), and *Cats Incredible* (Plume). He and his wife lecture widely on guardian angels and spirit guides. They appear frequently on television and radio, including "Entertainment Tonight" and "Hard Copy." They live in Forest City, Iowa.

GUARDIAN
ANGELS
AND SPIRIT
GUIDES

*True Accounts of Benevolent
Beings from the Other Side*

BRAD STEIGER

A PLUME BOOK

PLUME
Published by the Penguin Group
Penguin Books USA Inc., 375 Hudson Street,
New York, New York 10014, U. S. A.
Penguin Books Ltd, 27 Wrights Lane, London W8 5TZ, England
Penguin Books Australia Ltd, Ringwood, Victoria, Australia
Penguin Books Canada Ltd, 10 Alcorn Avenue,
Toronto, Ontario, Canada M4V 3B2
Penguin Books (N.Z.) Ltd, 182–190 Wairau Road, Auckland 10, New Zealand

Penguin Books Ltd, Registered Offices: Harmondsworth, Middlesex, England

First published by Plume, an imprint of Dutton Signet,
a division of Penguin Books USA Inc.

First Printing, January, 1995
10 9 8 7 6 5 4 3 2 1

 REGISTERED TRADEMARK—MARCA REGISTRADA

LIBRARY OF CONGRESS CATALOGING-IN-PUBLICATION DATA

Steiger, Brad.
Guardian angels and spirit guides : true accounts of benevolent beings from the
other side / Brad Steiger.
    p.   cm.
ISBN 0-452-27358-7
1. Guides (Spiritualism)   2. Guardian angels.   3. Spirits.   4. Ghosts.   I. Title
BF1275.G85S74   1995
291.2'15—dc20   94-19857
                                                                         CIP

Printed in the United States of America
Set in Garamond Light
Designed by Eve L. Kirch

BOOKS ARE AVAILABLE AT QUANTITY DISCOUNTS WHEN USED TO PROMOTE PRODUCTS OR SER-
VICES. FOR INFORMATION PLEASE WRITE TO PREMIUM MARKETING DIVISION, PENGUIN BOOKS USA
INC., 375 HUDSON STREET, NEW YORK, NEW YORK 10014.

CONTENTS

CONTENTS

Introduction: Someone Up There Likes Us!

Officer Christa Evans, a member of a major southern city's elite police department rescue squad, is but one of thousands of modern men and women who have learned through dramatic firsthand experience that the age-old promise that otherworldly beings are involved in the affairs of humans is as valid today as it was in the time of Abraham and Lot, Moses and Aaron, Jesus and the apostles. "Someone" up there, out there, or around a corner in another dimension is concerned about us, and whether we call them heavenly guides, guardian angels, or spirits of our dear departed ones does not really matter. What truly matters is that these entities seem to have the ability to appear when we need them the most.

Officer Evans had been diving in search of a woman who had driven her car off a ramp into the river. She quickly found the dazed motorist, pulled her free of the submerged car, and dragged her alive and sputtering to the surface. A waiting ambulance sped away to an emergency room with the fortunate woman, and it seemed as though the police rescue squad had successfully averted a tragic drowning.

But then a witness claimed that he had seen a passenger in the car with the driver before it sank.

"We had no prior report of another person in the car," said Officer Brian Curtis, Christa's partner. "Do you think this guy knows what he's talking about?"

"We can't take any chances," Christa answered. "I pulled the driver out from an air pocket trapped near the roof of the car. She was lucky I was able to get to her so fast. I didn't see anyone else down there."

"If there was," Officer Curtis observed solemnly, "he would surely have drowned by now."

Christa nodded in silent agreement. "Either way, I had better check it out. We can't risk leaving someone who might still be alive down there to drown. And in any event, it's my job to bring the victim to the surface."

"I wish the lady you just pulled out were still here to question," Officer Curtis said. "I hate to see you go down again so soon."

"She was dazed and in pretty bad shape," Christa reminded her partner. "We wouldn't have been able to rely on her memory. If there's any chance of anyone being left down there, I'd better dive immediately."

After several minutes of swimming around the submerged automobile, Christa satisfied herself that there was no other victim—alive or drowned—but she found herself in trouble when a sudden shift in water pressure slammed the car door shut on the little finger of her left hand.

With only a few minutes of air left in her tank, she frantically tried to open the door, but it would not budge. With her oxygen nearly gone, she knew that she must cut off her finger or drown.

"Please, dear God," she prayed, thinking especially of her two small children. "Please don't let me die like this."

According to Christa Evans, that was when a benevolent being appeared to rescue her: "A bright light approached me. It came within arm's length . . . and then it disappeared. But my finger was free! I rose to the surface and was pulled into a boat by two other members of the rescue squad. Neither of them had entered the water.

"I am convinced that it was my guardian angel that saved me from drowning."

If you believe in guardian angels, spirit guides, and benevolent beings from the Other Side, you stand in very good company.

Sir William Crookes, the great British chemist and physicist, was a firm believer in guidance from the spirit realm.

The Nobel prizewinning poet William Butler Yeats was outspoken in discussing his episodes of interaction with spirit entities.

Thomas A. Edison not only believed in guidance from the etheric realms but was working on an electronic apparatus to facilitate such contact at the time of his death.

Aviation pioneer Charles Lindbergh made his historic flight across the Atlantic together with etheric presences that helped guide him to safety.

Henry Ford, inventor and industrialist; publishing magnate William Randolph Hearst; military strategist General George S. Patton; and J. Paul Getty, the oil billionaire, all accepted the reality of guides and guardians from the Higher Realms.

Thousands of sober, sensible, responsible men and women have testified that they, too, have received the miracle of a helping hand from beyond.

Many people have told of having had their lives saved by the sudden materialization of someone who had passed on to the Other Side.

Other grateful recipients of spirit intervention tell of having been blessed with guidance when they were confused, with upliftment when they were mired in the depths of depression, or with direction when they felt lost on the pathway of life.

And there are others who swear that they were led to gold mines or to oil-bearing sites by materialized spirits of the deceased. Certain powerful and prosperous individuals give the full credit for the great wealth that they have amassed to the guidance that they have received from entities that exist in other dimensions of reality.

The skeptical will always have a ready answer to such dramatic accounts, and while it is certainly the right of the unrelenting cynics to hold such an unyielding materialistic interpretation of other people's miracles, they would be well advised not to voice such opinions too vociferously in the company of those whose lives have been saved or revitalized by the intercession of loving benefactors from beyond.

Father Andrew Greeley, who is a Ph.D. in sociology and a best-selling novelist as well as a Roman Catholic priest, has been keeping tabs on the paranormal experiences of Americans since 1973. Together with his colleagues at the University of Chicago, Dr. Greeley, a professor of sociology at the University of Arizona in Tucson, released the following data in the January/February 1987 issue of *American Health*:

- 73 percent of the adult population in the United States believe in life after death.
- 42 percent believe that they have been in contact with the dead, usually a deceased spouse or sibling.
- 74 percent expect to be reunited with their loved ones after death.

In the fall of 1988 the editors at *Better Homes and Gardens* decided to present a subject which they had never before touched: their readers' spiritual lives. They were amazed at both the quantity and the substance of the response to their survey.

"We reach thirty-six million readers each month," said editor in chief David Jordan. "Usually about twenty-five thousand respond to surveys we publish. But this subject drew more than eighty thousand responses, and more than ten thousand people attached thoughtful letters expressing remarkable strength of feeling. It is clearly a subject that strikes deeply at this time in our history."

Among the survey findings of *Better Homes and Gardens*, we find that of those eighty thousand readers who responded to the survey:

- 86 percent believe in miracles.
- 89 percent believe in eternal life.
- 30 percent perceive of a spirit world.
- 13 percent accept the possibility that beings in that spirit world make contact with the living.

A few years ago the scientific administration of public response polling that makes the Gallup poll so reliable in measuring the opinion of a mass audience found that 43 percent of U.S. citizens claim to have undergone an unusual spiritual experience and 71 percent believe in life after death.

On January 12, 1994, *USA TODAY* published the results of an analysis of the most recent comprehensive data available of private religious experience based on a national sociological survey conducted for the National Opinion Research Center, University of Chicago, which reveals that more than two thirds of Americans claim to have had at least one mystical experience.

- 67.3 percent say that they have experienced some form of extrasensory perception, such as telepathy, being in touch with someone who was far away from them.
- 28.3 percent claim an experience with clairvoyance, the ability to see events at a great distance as they happen.
- 39.9 percent are convinced that they have had contact with the dead.
- 31.5 percent have felt connected to a powerful spiritual force that seemed to elevate their consciousness.

Interestingly, according to the meticulous analysis of Jeffrey S. Levin, an associate professor at Eastern Virginia Medical School, Norfolk, Virginia, such experiences as the above are reported *less* by those people who are active in church or synagogue. All these types of mystical experiences have been around since "time immemorial," Levin acknowledges, but "some kind of stigma" may have prevented people from reporting them. However, while only 5 percent of the population has such experiences somewhat regularly, such occurrences are becoming "more common with each successive generation."

Since 1967 I have been interviewing men and women throughout the United States, Canada, Great Britain, Europe, and the Mideast who claim to have undergone some kind of "unusual spiritual experience." By this writing, in 1994, I have collected about thirty thousand questionnaires from the aforementioned interviewees, readers of my books, and those men and women who attend the lectures and seminars that I conduct with my wife, Sherry Hansen Steiger.

Of those thirty thousand percipients of paranormal experiences:

- 48 percent are convinced that they have seen a ghost.
- 42 percent believe that they have seen and interacted with the spirit of a departed loved one.
- 38 percent report the visitation of an angelic being.
- 50 percent are convinced that they have received guidance and/or protection from a spirit being or a guardian angel.
- 55 percent feel certain that they have received some form of communication from deceased friends or relatives.
- 55 percent have had a near-death experience.

In my opinion, the results of the above-mentioned polls and surveys clearly indicate that large numbers of men and women believe that we have within each of us a soul, an external spark of divinity that is not trapped in the same cycle that imprisons the atoms of hydrogen and oxygen. Such expressions of belief give evidence of a quenchless inner conviction that we are something more than an arrangement of biochemical compounds, that we are children of God, rather than cousins of the laboratory guinea pig.

Guardian Angels and Spirit Guides contains many true, documented accounts of men and women who know with complete certainty that they have received invaluable assistance from benevolent beings from the other side.

Not only do these remarkable stories tell of lives saved, renewed, or redeemed, but the very testimonies of those who have interacted with caring entities from beyond constitute dramatic, undeniable proof of the continuance of life after death.

GUARDIAN ANGELS
AND SPIRIT GUIDES

1. Warning Voices from an Unseen World

According to a recent poll conducted by a national newsmagazine (*Time,* December 27, 1993), 69 percent of Americans believe in the existence of angels, and 46 percent maintain that they have their own guardian angels to watch over them and to guide them.

Of those men and women polled by the magazine, 32 percent claim that they have personally felt the presence and/or guidance of ethereal entities in their lives, and 15 percent believe that the heavenly helpers that ministered to them were the benevolent spirits of people who had died, rather than higher spiritual beings with special powers.

There is a provocative scene in the motion picture *Grand Canyon* in which Kevin Kline, who plays a harried Los Angeles businessman on his way to a meeting on Wilshire Boulevard's "Miracle Mile," carelessly steps off the curb while absorbed in anxious thoughts about the approaching encounter. A stranger grabs him and yanks him back—he tells a friend—"just as a city bus went flying by my nose."

Suddenly very much aware that he could easily have become a "wet bug stain on the front of the bus," he turns around to thank the person who saved him and glimpses what appears to be a young woman wearing a Pittsburgh Pirates cap rapidly fading into the crowd. The Pirates, we learn, has been his favorite baseball team since childhood.

Reflecting on the true nature of his anonymous rescuer, Kline's character wonders: "Was that a real person? Or was that something else—you know—sent from somewhere else?"

Like the character in *Grand Canyon,* I have often wondered if that *something* else that on occasion chooses to help us out of a terrible dilemma or what would appear to be a fatal accident—thereby postponing our demise for a later date—conducts its act of intercession as part of a heavenly mission or as a sustained interest in the affairs of humans.

To ask the question another way, are our heavenly helpers angelic messengers of God who intercede for us as a function of their divine assignment, or are our benevolent intercessors the spirits of deceased human beings who wish to assist those of us still in the flesh to attain higher states of peace, love, and awareness?

To ponder the matter further still, it may be that on certain occasions angelic beings deliberately assume the images of the dearly departed in order to perform more effectively their mission on Earth. If someone in need of guidance will respond more rapidly to the ghost of Uncle Charlie bringing a message of warning, then an angelic messenger may assume such a form in order to sound the alarm and get the job done as quickly and efficiently as possible.

Of course, all of the above discussion is entirely academic to those who have had their lives saved by the dramatic intercession of an entity—be it angel or spirit—who chose to become involved in the course of human events.

* * *

Elizabeth Muller recalled the time when she was a girl of around seven helping her father, mother, two older brothers, and some neighbors pick blackberries on their farm in Arkansas. The berries were plentiful that year, and she had been given a small bucket to carry the succulent fruit back to a larger basket.

"Don't you lollygag none, Liz," her mother warned her. "There's lots of chores to do yet today, so we want to finish up this job in a hurry."

Since she was smaller and had to take her time to avoid the stab of the prickly briers, little Liz decided to find a patch of her own where the older berry pickers wouldn't rush her so.

"I had just started to push my way into the thicket where the berries were most plentiful when I heard a voice shout at me, 'Don't go in there, Liz! Back away!' " Elizabeth said.

"I was really startled, because the voice sounded just like Grandma Hankins, who had died that winter at the age of eighty-six. But I looked around and saw nobody near me.

"I knew it couldn't be Grandma Hankins, so then I thought maybe it might be Chaw, my younger brother, disguising his voice to tease me, to scare me so I wouldn't pick many berries and he could make fun of me, so I started to push into the briers to go after the blackberries."

This time the voice was louder, sterner, more formal: *"Elizabeth,* you get away from there. There's a big rattlesnake in there, and it will bite you!"

Elizabeth said that the second time the voice really got her attention with its talk of a rattlesnake. "Plus the fact that when I was a little kid, no one ever called me Elizabeth except Mom or Grandma Hankins when they got really cross with me.

"I ran toward my parents and brothers and told them to

come quick with their hoes. I told them that there was a big, *really big* rattlesnake in my berry patch.

"At first Mom just scolded me for telling a tale, thinking that I was making up a story to get out of picking berries, but Dad told my brothers to go check it out.

"Pretty soon the boys were yelling and chopping away like mad in the midst of my berry patch.

"When they came back out, they dragged a dead rattle-snake behind them. It had fifteen rattles on its tail. That is a *big* rattlesnake!

"The voice had saved my life. It had told the truth. There really was a big rattlesnake just waiting for me in the berry patch."

An account of a warning voice that saved a husband and wife from fatal injury was told to me not long ago when a group of friends shared their experiences of unusual events in their lives.

George Hansen remembered the Christmas holidays in 1956, when he and his wife, Eleanor, were visiting his mother on the old homeplace in southern Wisconsin.

"Dad had passed away the preceding Christmas," George said, "and Mom lived alone in the farmhouse. Her brother, my uncle Leonard, farmed the land. Eleanor and I were joining my sisters, Klara and Sal, and their husbands on the family farm for the traditional holiday feast and gift exchange, with the ulterior motive of convincing our mother to leave the farm and move into an apartment in town.

"We still had the '48 Ford coupe at that time, and the old bucket of bolts was notorious for dying and stalling at the most inopportune moments. We were driving toward the family farm on a cold, starless night when the Ford's motor died about a mile and a half from our destination."

George managed to glide the car a bit closer to the side of the two-lane blacktop before it came to a complete halt.

"Wonderful!" Eleanor said, shaking her head bitterly. "This is just wonderful. Now we have to carry our luggage over a mile to the farmhouse. And I'm in high heels besides!"

George knew his wife could get frostbitten toes hiking through the snow on such a cold night. "You stay in the car," he told her. "I'll walk to the farm, get a tractor from the shed, and pull us to the house."

"Be careful. Don't slip on the icy spots, honey," Eleanor warned him as he got out of the coupe.

George appreciated her concern, but he knew by the way that she draped the travel blanket around her exposed toes that he had responded in the manner that she had hoped.

When he got out of the coupe, he saw that there was a slight downward incline just a few yards ahead of him. It might not be necessary for either one of them to walk to the farmhouse.

"Sweetie," he said, opening the door to announce his discovery, "if I can push the car just a few yards to an incline up ahead, I think we can jump-start the engine. So you steer while I push."

Eleanor slid over behind the steering wheel and pushed in the clutch. She was to keep the clutch to the floorboard until the Ford picked up speed, then take her foot off the clutch and hope that the coupe jumped back to life. She was quite familiar with the procedure from her having been in the car on countless prior occasions when its engine had died.

George had just got the Ford rolling, and he had stepped to the rear to give it his solid shoulder from behind.

"I was pushing against the rear of the coupe with all my strength when I heard my father's voice shout at me to jump in the ditch," George said. "As clear as could be, with the slight Swedish accent that he had never managed to lose, I heard Dad yell, 'George, get out of the way! Jump in the ditch . . . now!' "

George was in the process of obeying the urging of his father's bodiless voice when a car, speeding so fast that neither he nor Eleanor had seen its approach from the rear, slammed into the back of the '48 Ford coupe.

"I was not quite fast enough," George said. "The Plymouth sedan struck my hip a glancing blow and tossed me into the ditch, where I lapsed into unconsciousness."

When he awakened in the hospital, George was informed that he had suffered a broken leg, a fractured hip, and numerous bruises.

"Although I spent a couple of weeks in the hospital and it took months for all of my injuries to heal, I know that if it had not been for the warning shout of my father's voice, I would have been crushed and almost certainly killed by the force of the Plymouth sedan smashing me against our Ford coupe," George said.

Eleanor had suffered only a few cuts and bruises, for she, too, had heard the warning voice of her deceased father-in-law.

Startled into instant obedience by the sound of a voice from beyond the grave, she had jumped from the front seat of the coup into the ditch. The impact of the sedan striking the rear of their Ford had served as an additional impetus to project her free of the violent crash.

Fortunately the teenaged couple driving the Plymouth also survived the accident with a number of minor concussions, breaks, and bruises.

"Eleanor and I both heard quite clearly the warning shout of my father, and we both recognized the distinctive voice as belonging to my dad," George said.

"In addition to his warning voice having saved our lives, it was so reassuring to us at that time, when Dad had been gone for just one year, to know that his spiritual presence was still with us and looking after us.

"Mother joined him two years later. Eleanor passed on in 1987, and now that I am seventy-two years old, I know that it may not be long before we will all be together again."

The major world religions are in accord concerning one great teaching: that human beings are immortal, that there is a spirit within each of us that may return to its place of origin in a divine world. The affirmation that death is not the end constitutes the one promise that the many religious sects with their diversity of beliefs hold in common.

Episcopal Bishop Philip Brooks once thoughtfully observed that there is nothing clearer or more striking in the Bible "than the calm, familiar way with which from end to end it assumes the present existence of a world of spiritual beings always close to and acting on this world of flesh and blood. . . .

"From creation to judgment, the spiritual beings are forever present. They act as truly in the drama as the men and women who, with their unmistakable humanity, walk the sacred stage in successive scenes. There is nothing of hesitation about the Bible's treatment of the spiritual world. There is no reserve, no vagueness which would leave a chance for the whole system to be explained away in dreams and metaphors. The spiritual world, with all its multitudinous existence, is just as real as the crowded cities and the fragrant fields and the loud battle-grounds of the visible, palpable Judea, in which the writers of the sacred books were living."

2. An Invisible Entity Saved Her Baby's Life

One of the wonderful perks inherent in the business of being a writer is that you are likely to run across a good story wherever you roam—and sometimes in the most unlikely places. Since we travel a great deal gathering research materials and conducting seminars, we are continually being presented with excellent material for our files and subsequent books.

In early November of 1989 Sherry and I were invited to Vancouver, British Columbia, to serve as guest panelists on the television talk show *Beyond the Line*. Overall, the experience was very enjoyable, and it was made all the more pleasant by our stay in a deluxe guest room at the lovely Meridien Hotel. As yet another marvelous bonus, we were told the following story of how instructions spoken by an unseen voice saved an infant's life.

In August 1967 Diana Chapman's husband, James, and two of his coworkers from the insurance office had left on a long fishing weekend, leaving her home with their five-year-old son, Joel, and two-year-old son, Dean.

At that time the Chapmans lived in a duplex next to a city park with a great many trees and well-kept lawns. Diana enjoyed strolling with the children in the park, and the first two days of her husband's absence passed without incident.

A person who lived most comfortably according to a regular schedule, Diana would feed the children promptly at 5:00 P.M., allow them to play or watch television until precisely 7:15, when she would bathe them so they might be in bed by 8:00.

"On this particular night, since it was very warm outside, the boys chose to sit quietly and watch cartoons on television," Diana recalled. "They were unusually quiet while I tidied up the kitchen, and I had just mentally been remarking that generally speaking, we had been blessed with trouble-free children.

"I was just putting away the last of the dinner dishes when little Dean staggered into the kitchen with his arms outstretched toward me. His eyes were wide with fear and obvious discomfort, and his mouth was opening and closing, making gasping and sucking sounds, as if he were having trouble breathing properly."

Diana rushed to Dean and knelt to take him in her arms. "What is it, honey? Can you tell Mommy what's wrong?"

As she began to lift the child, he suddenly went limp in her arms.

"I kept telling myself not to panic," Diana said, "but what can frighten a mother more than her baby suddenly losing consciousness with her not knowing the cause?"

Diana loosened Dean's clothing, then examined his head for any bumps or bruises.

"When I found no physical marks of any kind, I really started to become frightened," Diana said. "I didn't know what to do.

"I called Joel into the room and as calmly as possible asked him if he knew what was the matter with his brother. He just stared at me blankly and shook his head in the negative."

Diana carried Dean to the sink to wash his face and head with cool water. If that didn't bring him around, she resolved to take no further chances. She would call the doctor immediately.

Diana was nearly to the sink when she felt a stinging slap on her back. Startled, she turned around to see nothing or no one who could have dealt her such a sharp blow.

"But it was at that point that I distinctly heard a deep masculine voice ordering me to turn Dean upside down and to place my finger down his throat," Diana said. "Stunned, confused, wondering if stress was causing me to lose my mind, I stood there immobile, helplessly clutching Dean to my chest."

Two more smart slaps stung her shoulder and brought her out of her temporary paralysis.

"Quickly!" the voice demanded. "If you wish to save your son's life, hold his head down and put your finger down his throat!"

Diana felt weak, dizzy. Could such things really be happening to her?

Yet another powerful, stinging slap on her shoulder emphasized the urgency of the voice's commands: "Hurry! To save your son's life, you must act now!"

Prodded at last into obedience by the demands of the stern voice and the smart blows on her shoulder, Diana turned baby Dean over her knee with his head down and stuck her finger down his throat.

She managed to dislodge a pink lump of the children's clay that she had always feared might smell and taste too good to remain simply something to be molded and not eaten.

Little Dean sucked in a deep gasp of air and began to cry. Diana sobbed with relief that the crisis seemed to have passed and that her baby appeared to be all right.

"When Dean's lusty screams had been reduced to soft whimpers, I once again had the presence of mind to look about the kitchen, seeking some clue to the source of the remarkable experience with the unseen voice that had saved my child's life," Diana said.

"I asked Joel—who had stood in the kitchen throughout the entire episode, watching the drama play itself out as if he were transfixed—if he had heard a voice talking to me. I mean, the commands were so loud and clear I would have suspected our neighbors in the duplex might have heard them."

Diana recalled that Joel shook his head and replied, "No, Mommy. There is no one here besides me, and I was too scared to say anything!"

Later that night, as she prepared for bed, Diana remained baffled by the sound of the mysterious voice and the impact of the stinging blows from an invisible hand.

"I was about to step into the tub for a good, hot bath when I was astonished to see quite clearly a series of reddened, weltlike marks across my shoulders. Hours later I could still distinguish the imprints of what certainly appeared to be human fingers in the flesh of my back."

Diana fell asleep that night with fervent prayers of thanks on her lips. She knew that the voice had saved her son's life, and she did not begrudge *whomever* the stinging slaps that had prompted her into action and into obedience.

When James returned the next afternoon, his catch of fish and the stories that accompanied each marine trophy paled into insignificance when Diana told him of the miraculous rescue of their son by an unseen entity.

"Although James has never been a particularly religious man," Diana said, "he told me that he firmly believed that the voice that I had heard belonged to Dean's guardian angel. James said that in his opinion, it simply wasn't our baby's time to return to Heaven, and his angel saw to it that he be granted a longer period of time on Earth to learn and to grow."

3. The Ghost of Their Mother Waved Them Back from Danger

Susan Barenburg of Salem, Oregon, lost her mother when she was just a young girl of ten and the family was living in Yreka, California.

"I was terribly despondent over the loss of Mom, and the other kids and Dad were taking her death just as hard as I was," she said.

"There were four of us kids. I was second oldest. Debra was twelve, Paula was eight, and Douglas was six. We all cried ourselves to sleep every night for weeks after Mom's funeral in March 1973. We could hear Daddy crying in his room, too. We all just missed Mom too much."

Susan's father stuck it out until school was dismissed for the summer; then he decided that it would be best for the entire family if they moved to another town and made a fresh start. There were just too many memories of Mom in Yreka, he told the children. It would be easier for all of them to get on with their lives if they weren't thinking about her all of the time.

"Dad decided that we should try a whole different lifestyle while we were at it," Susan said. "He had heard about this old farmhouse outside a small town in Oregon, and he thought that we should check it out."

The kids took one look at the ramshackle house and started to pray that their father wouldn't like it.

"It was big enough," Susan recalled. "It had six bedrooms, a large country kitchen, and a neat living room with window boxes. The problem was, it was really run-down and needed a lot of fixing up. Debra and I knew that Mom's illness had cost Dad a lot of money. And then, of course, there had been the funeral expenses. While the low asking price might appeal to Dad's busted budget, we hoped that he would realize how much money we would have to spend to fix the place up to make it really livable."

Paula and little Doug were excited about the large barn and the various outbuildings and animal sheds. They began immediately to dream about having horses to ride.

While their father discussed terms with the landlord, the kids set off on a tour of inspection of the old, sprawling house.

"We had already decided which one of us got which room," Susan said. "And we had even climbed the dusty steps to the walk-up attic and found some potential treasure chests of old clothes and hats that some family had left behind. They would be just great for playing dress-up."

The four children had scampered helter-skelter from room to room until only the basement remained for them to explore.

"I don't like basements," Paula protested, hanging back.

"Why not?" Debra wanted to know.

"Because they're dark and smelly and spooky," Paula replied with hesitation.

"And monsters live under the stairs!" little Douglas added, his large blue eyes growing even wider at the thought of braving the basement.

"Oh, pooh, you guys." Susan teased them. "Don't be little sissies. Let's explore the basement. I'll bet we'll find some neat things that someone has left down there."

"You go ahead." Paula was adamant. "Dougie and I will stay upstairs."

"If we're going to live here," Debra told them, "you can't be afraid to go down in the cellar."

Paula could not suppress an involuntary shudder. "Oh, I hope we don't have to live in this creepy old place."

"That's for Dad to decide," Debra reminded her. "Come on, now, I'll take Douglas's hand, and Paula, you take Susan's hand, and we will all run down the basement stairs together. You can't be afraid if we are all together."

Reluctantly Paula and Douglas did as they were told, and each took the hand of an older sister.

"We were about halfway down the stairs when we all came to a sudden stop," Susan said. "There at the bottom of the stairs was Mom!"

In her written report Susan stated that all the children had clearly seen an image of their deceased mother, and each of them described her in the same way.

"She had on this really pretty sundress with big flowers on it that all of us kids loved so much," Susan said. "Her long blond hair was braided, like she often fixed it in the warm weather.

"But most of all, we all saw her beautiful smile. She was smiling up at us so lovingly. I will never forget the image of the way that I saw her that day."

The children probably would have run into the arms of their lovely, smiling mother if she had not begun to make motions that they should go back up the stairs, that they should not continue their route to the basement.

"When Paula went down a couple more steps toward her, Mom frowned and made a motion that Paula should stop. I know that we were all probably crying and calling out to her and saying that we wanted to hug and kiss her, but she kept waving her arms and motioning us to go back."

Just when the children appeared to act as though they might ignore her gestures and proceed down the steps toward her, the image of their mother disappeared.

"We ran upstairs to get Dad and to tell him that we had seen Mom at the bottom of the basement stairs," Susan said. "Since we were all crying and talking at the same time, he could hardly ignore us or argue that we were *all* seeing things."

When the landlord, an elderly man in his mid-eighties, finally understood that the children were talking excitedly about something in the cellar, he became very agitated.

"No, no, you mustn't let those kids go down in the basement!" he said extra loud because of his partial deafness. "There's an old cistern down there right at the bottom of the stairs. The boards have rotted away, and I'll have to fix it before anyone goes down there."

Dad was shocked that the landlord hadn't mentioned such a potential danger spot immediately, but it was easy to see that the elderly gentleman had trouble keeping his mind on more than one thing at a time. And he had quite obviously forgotten long ago how young children will want to explore old houses when given the opportunity.

"When Dad went to investigate, he found things exactly as the old man had described them," Susan said. "The cistern, a deep and open uncovered well with about a foot of water in the bottom, was right in the dark at the bottom of the basement stairs. The way that we kids were running hand in hand down those stairs we all would have fallen into the well and probably have been killed."

Susan concluded her account by stating that her father had decided on the spot against renting the old farmhouse and that he never once doubted the children when they told him that their beautiful mother had returned with her loving smile to save their lives.

"Because she was the one who gave you life in the first place," her father said, "it surely does stand to reason that she would do her best to protect your lives even from beyond the grave."

Then, Susan added, her father got tears in his eyes and said, "Now you kids know for certain that love never dies."

4. The Father Who Came Back to Protect His Family

Not long ago, after one of our seminars in San Diego, Margaret Glasson told Sherry and me this fascinating account of her deceased husband's continued interest in his family.

"I was half asleep one night, reading the newspaper in my reclining chair in the front room, when I thought I heard Cissy, my three-year-old daughter, whimpering in her bedroom," Margaret said.

"About the same time I heard the trash can in back of the house go clattering into the alley. Cautiously I peeped out a window in the kitchen and caught a glimpse of a man standing in the shadows beside the garage."

Margaret did her best to quiet the trembling fear that seized her. Taking a deep breath to center herself, she walked purposefully back into the front room and called the police.

"I sat in my easy chair, using all of my willpower to retain control, praying earnestly that a police car would pull up in the alley before I could count ten.

"Then I heard my little girl whimpering once again. Sud-

denly a new terror seized me and sent my heart pounding:
What if there was already an intruder *inside* the house?"

Margaret opened the door to Cissy's bedroom and was unable to suppress the cry of horror that escaped her lips when
she saw a man leaning over her daughter's bed.

Her brain struggled with a hundred different fears. She was
alone. The police were nowhere in sight. Did the intruder
mean to hurt her child?

But then, to her complete amazement, she heard the man
singing softly to Cissy.

Within another moment or two she was able to focus her
senses sharply enough to recognize the tune of an old lullaby
that had been a favorite of her husband's.

"Who—who are you?" she asked the man. He had drawn
the hood of a sweatshirt over his face so that she could not
distinguish any of his features in the dim light of the child's
bedroom.

"Who are you?" she repeated, trying to dismiss all inflec-
tions of fear from her voice.

As the man raised his head and turned to face her, Margaret
was startled to see the face of her husband, William. In the
next instant the image vanished.

"I was about to collapse, but that's when the police officer
knocked on the front door," Margaret said.

"He was just checking to see if everything was all right, and
he told me that they had picked up a man just leaving the alley in back of the house that they immediately recognized as
a known burglar. According to the officer, the man had a rap
sheet of prior offenses as long as his arm."

Margaret thanked the officer for the quick work in appre-
hending a criminal who quite obviously had scheduled her
house as one of his targets for the night.

"Glad to be of service, ma'am," he said, "but you are extremely lucky that your husband was at home with you to-night."

"My husband?" Margaret echoed hollowly.

"Yes," the officer went on. "You see, most burglars just like to slip in and out of a house without even being seen, but this man is different. He's got a real sadistic streak. If he should happen to see a woman home alone, he doesn't mind break-ing in and hurting her while he loots the place. And if there should happen to be a youngster around, he doesn't hesitate at all to beat up the kid, too."

"The burglar said that he saw my husband in the house?" Margaret had to ask for confirmation of what she herself had witnessed in Cissy's bedroom just before the officer had knocked on the door.

"Yeah, the guy said that he kept peeping in your windows, but he always saw this big man standing right beside your chair.

"A couple of times he went around to try to enter through the child's bedroom, but then he saw your husband in there, bending over your daughter's bed, singing to her.

"He said your husband had on a hooded sweatshirt like he had been working out or something. So it's a good thing he was home tonight."

The officer frowned quizzically, glanced around the front room. "Where is your husband now? Did he go to bed or something?"

"Officer," Margaret answered, "my husband, William, died nearly two years ago. He and a couple of his buddies were out fishing when a sudden storm came up. William fell over-board. His body was never recovered. It is quite likely, though, that he was wearing a hooded sweatshirt that night, too."

The officer became very quiet, excused himself, said good-night, and left.

"I don't know if he believed me or not," Margaret said. "I really didn't care.

"I knew that William's great love for us had drawn him back to protect us on the night when we were threatened by a man who would have stolen our valuables and harmed us physically.

"And I will never forget the glimpse that I received of him in Cissy's room or the beautiful sound of his singing his favorite lullaby over his daughter's sleeping form.

"In addition to saving us from pain and theft, William gave us the greatest gift imaginable: proof that there is life and love beyond the grave."

5. The Warning Voice of Her Dead Husband Saved Her Life

Seventy-one-year-old Kristin Forbeck had been sleeping soundly in her comfortable two-bedroom cabin on the shore of a northern Minnesota lake when she distinctly heard the voice of her husband, David, calling her name.

"I was awakened from a sound sleep," Kristin wrote in a lengthy, detailed letter in March 1992. "I remember that I sat up in bed and fumbled for the light, glancing wildly about the dark room as I did so. I knew with every fiber of my being that I had not been mistaken about the source of the voice. I would forever recognize the sound of my beloved David's voice—even though he had been taken from me by a heart attack five years before."

Kristin finally managed to locate the light switch, and she got out of bed, sliding her feet into warm slippers. It was a chilly night in late November, and she knew the floorboards would be cold.

"Kristin." The voice spoke again, seemingly just over her right shoulder. "Look sharp, girl. Something is burning! You are in danger, my beloved."

She spun around, hoping to catch at least a fleeting glimpse of her husband's spirit.

"I saw nothing. But the voice was so distinctly David's. And years ago, after we had been amused by a British movie in which a military man had always prefaced his commands with a snappy 'look sharp,' we had used the phrase teasingly whenever we wanted the other to get right at a domestic chore."

Kristin pulled on a robe. The cabin's furnace was run by electricity, and she had adjusted the thermostat before retiring. She knew that she had not left on any electrical appliance, such as a toaster or an iron. Perhaps she had only been dreaming after all.

"David had been almost phobic about the idea of our house burning," Kristin said. "His maternal aunt's house had caught fire when he had been just a boy. The lovely old house had burned to the ground, but even worse, his favorite cousin, Katy, had been horribly burned and left badly scarred.

"Once, three or four years after we were married in 1943, David had awakened in the night and found some trash smoldering in the kitchen wastebasket.

"He was mortified when he discovered that he had carelessly dumped an ashtray with a live butt into the trash, and he was horrified when he considered that he could have been responsible for setting our house on fire. He had become even more fearful of fire, and he quit smoking, cold turkey, that very night."

As she made her way into the living room to investigate further, Kristin pondered these things and began to consider quite strongly that her mind might have played back a kind of mental tape of David's voice.

She heard a noise in the backyard and looked out a window to see a graceful family of deer moving down toward the lake. An owl hooted mournfully from somewhere deep in the forest. All was peaceful and as it should be. She had only awakened from a strangely vivid dream.

"As if in answer to my mental debate and its rational conclusion, I heard David's voice once again," Kristin said. "This time the message was brief and forceful: 'The cabin is on fire!' "

Becoming even more confused and not a little frightened, Kristin walked from room to room in the ranch-style cabin.

Nothing!

She could find no sign of any threatening flames.

"Earlier, while I had taken my nightcap of warm cocoa, I had built a nice, crackling wood fire in the fireplace," Kristin said. "The fire had burned out hours ago. There were only a few still-glowing embers visible behind the fire screen."

Fire!

David's voice was insistent, demanding.

Kristin began to cry in frustration. "Where?" she asked. "Please tell me where!

"I leaned back against the wall next to the brick chimney in a state of seeming near collapse," Kristin said. "And, then, suddenly, I felt that the wall was hot.

"When I turned to place my open palm against the wall, I was horrified to find that it was extremely hot to the touch. Through a tiny crack between the fireplace mantel and the wall, I could see raging flames. The house was on fire!"

Kristin forced herself to remain as calm as possible and to head for the telephone in the kitchen and to dial 911.

"Although the village was small, it had an excellent volunteer fire department," she said. "I knew that they would get to me as quickly as possible.

"After I cradled the receiver, it seemed as though I had at last become truly wide-awake. I could now hear quite clearly the terrible, crackling sound of the fire spreading toward the roof. Tendrils of dark smoke were moving across the living room like greedy fingers of the fire seeking objects for consumption.

"I decided it would be safer to await the fire department in the yard, and even as I was pulling on a heavy coat to wear over my robe, I could hear the eerie wail of a siren shrilling a summons to the volunteer firemen.

" 'Thank you, David,' I said to the stars. 'Thank you, my darling, for saving my life.' "

Kristin said that the prompt action of the local firefighters prevented the complete destruction of her cabin, but the estimated cost of the repairs played a major factor in her decision to move into an apartment in a nearby larger city.

"I miss the solitude of our cabin by the lake," she said, "but I sense strongly that David's spirit feels better now that I am nearer our friends and family and not so lonely. Besides, there is a fire station only two blocks away."

6. A Light Being Kept Her Away from a Rapist

In 1976 an extensive survey conducted by the Gallup poll people indicated that 31 percent of Americans had experienced an "otherworldly" feeling of union with a Divine Being. Interpreted in numbers of adults, this percentage would represent approximately forty-seven million people.

The survey was based on in-home interviews with adults in more than three hundred scientifically selected localities across the nation, and a further breakdown of the percentages revealed that 34 percent of the women polled and 27 percent of the men admitted that they had had "a religious experience."

To refute the often heard suggestion that people with little formal education are more likely to undergo such experiences, the poll disclosed little difference in the educational level of the respondents: college background, 29 percent; high school, 31 percent; grade school, 30 percent.

According to the administrators of the poll, "Whether one regards these experiences as in the nature of self-delusion or wishful thinking, the important fact remains that, for the per-

sons concerned, such experiences are very real and meaning-
ful.

"Most important, perhaps, is the finding that these religious
experiences are widespread and not limited to particular
groups [or] one's circumstances in life . . . rich or poor, educa-
ted or uneducated, churched or unchurched."

According to a press release issued by the Gallup office in
Princeton, New Jersey, these kinds of experiences "appear to
have a profound effect on the outlook and direction of a person's life."

A twenty-nine-year-old office worker in Lynnwood, Wash-
ington, told a Gallup interviewer that she had been reading
the Bible one night and was unable to sleep. A vision appeared to her that rendered her frozen, motionless.

"I saw an unusual light that wasn't there—but was," she
said. "There was a greater awareness of someone else being
in that room with me. And ever since, it is as if someone else
is walking with me."

According to a spokesperson for the Gallup poll, "One of
the most interesting aspects of these phenomena is that they
happen to the nonchurched and the nonreligious as well as to
persons who attend church regularly or who say religion plays
an important role in their lives."

Although Dorothy Benner had never been much of a
churchgoer or at all inclined to be religious, her lifesaving encounter with a powerful Light Being when she was a young
married woman brought her into a new state of awareness
and grace.

"My experience with the heavenly being took place just a
few months after I married David in 1970," she said. "We
didn't have much money in those days, and we lived in a
pretty rough section of Kansas City. When we moved into the

third house in a run-down string of five that had all been built just alike sometime around the turn of the century, we kept telling ourselves that one day we would have it better."

Dorothy usually got home from her job as a waitress about two hours before David came home from the factory where he worked. David said that it was humiliating that she had to do such menial work. In his family tradition the man of the family had always supported his wife. Although he gave in to her working to help them achieve a better life faster, he insisted that because of the rough neighborhood, she must be home before dark. To make matters even worse, the young women in their section of Kansas City had been the target of a rapist-slasher who had already killed one unfortunate victim and cut and raped at least a dozen others.

Three nights a week David went right to night school after work, so she had to keep his dinner warm until after ten o'clock. It was tough on both of them, but they understood that those business courses that David was taking would eventually prove to be their ticket to better times.

"It was on a chilly October night that the incident occurred," Dorothy said. "David was still at school, and I was keeping his dinner warm in the kitchen.

"I was relaxing in the living room by putting my bare feet up on a footstool and reading a new book. I didn't expect David for at least another hour, and it felt so good after being on my feet all day just to sit and take it easy for a while. At about ten minutes to nine, though, I thought it was time to check David's meal to be certain it didn't dry out.

"When I reached the door between the living room and the kitchen, I was suddenly stopped dead in my tracks by some invisible force that prevented me from passing through the doorway," Dorothy explained. "Some unseen, solid barrier that I could actually feel pressing against my chest and arms was holding me back."

Stunned, doubting her own senses, Dorothy lunged toward the doorway with all of her strength. She was thrown back with such force that she lost her balance and dropped to one knee.

"I have always been a tall woman, standing just over five feet ten," she said. "I was just twenty-two at the time of the occurrence, very athletic, solidly built, weighing about one hundred and forty pounds. I had grown up on a Missouri farm doing a man's work, and I was completely shaken by the experience of being knocked to my knees by something I couldn't see."

Dorothy slumped against the side of the sofa and studied the open doorway. She doesn't really remember how long she sat there trying to figure out what it was that had prevented her from entering the kitchen.

"The doorway was clear. I could see absolutely nothing that could have blocked my path to the kitchen," she said. "So I got back up and rushed the doorway once again."

This time she experienced the flash of a brilliant blue light as she struck the impenetrable invisible barrier, and she felt a fairly powerful electric type of shock that knocked her back on her posterior.

"I shook my head to clear it of fear and confusion," she said. "I tried to center myself and focus on the impossible scene that had suddenly begun to play itself out in our home.

"When I looked up once again to confront the open doorway, I saw a blue light shimmering there. For just a few seconds the light took the shape of a tall, powerfully built man, and then it faded away."

Awestruck by the manifestation of the Light Being, Dorothy got slowly to her feet and approached the doorway. "This time I gingerly poked a finger in the air and saw the blue light manifest again. As incredible as it may seem, I saw my fingertip rest lightly against the dimly defined upraised palm of a big man composed entirely of shimmering blue light.

"When I tried to pass through the doorway, the Light Being's palm moved from my fingertip to my chest, and once again I felt it push me back into the living room."

When the telephone on the end table began to ring, Dorothy was so startled she felt as though she had jumped to the ceiling. It probably rang four or five times before she had the presence of mind to answer it.

"Dorothy, it's your next-door neighbor, Pearl," the voice told her. "You just listen carefully to what I am about to say. You know that these five houses in a row are all built just exactly alike, so I know just where your telephone is. You just sit there and talk to me and don't move away from the sofa."

Dorothy's head was swimming. First an entity made of blue light blocked her path to the kitchen and now her next-door neighbor was telling her not to move from the telephone.

Pearl kept her voice low, but her words were beginning to gain powerful vibrancy and meaning. "Now, don't you be afraid, but I can see a man standing right outside your kitchen door. He's got a big butcher knife in his hand, and it is plain to see that he has been waiting for you to come back into the kitchen."

Dorothy could not suppress a gasp of horror. She felt a cold sweat break out over her entire body.

"Now don't you go screaming or being afraid, girl," Pearl said sternly. "He can't see you there on your sofa when you talk on the telephone, so you just stay there!"

"But—but he has a *knife?*" Dorothy asked in a hoarse whisper. "Do you think . . . that he—"

"I think he might be the rapist-slasher all right," Pearl said matter-of-factly, "so you just sit tight. I called the police the second I spotted him walking up our back alley."

Just then, in answer to Dorothy's unspoken prayer, the

sound of police sirens cut through the heavy atmosphere of fear and confusion.

"Praise Jesus," Pearl said, "I can hear the police cars coming right now! You just sit tight, honey, until they come into your house."

Pearl hung up her phone, and Dorothy remained frozen in place until almost simultaneously with the knocking on her front door she heard the sound of scuffling and shouts outside the kitchen.

"Poor David came home just as the police were leading away in handcuffs the man who had been waiting outside our kitchen to attack me," Dorothy said. "The way David came bursting into the house all trembling and shaking with tears in his eyes told me far more than words could say that he really loved me."

The next evening's paper was full of the account of how the police had apprehended the notorious slasher-rapist because of an alert woman's telephone call.

"When I told David about my incredible experience with the Light Being that would not permit me to enter the kitchen, we both knew that my life had been saved because of its actions," Dorothy said.

"David said that it had to have been my guardian angel protecting me, and I had to agree. 'Someone up there *really* likes you,' he said.

"Although I had only gone to church once in a while, like at Christmastime and Easter, since I had been baptized, I became a regular churchgoer after that experience," Dorothy said. "I have found a real strength in knowing that there are Heavenly beings somewhere out there who really care for us."

7. How the Traditional Native American Medicine Teachings Regard the Spirit Guardian

When Chief Seathe (Seattle) learned that the white man had cheated his people out of their lands with the Treaty of Point Elliott in 1855, he pronounced a prophetic warning that the white conquerors would always have to deal with the red man—if not in the flesh, then as phantoms:

"Our religion is the traditions of our ancestors, the dreams of our old men, given them by the Great Spirit, and the visions of our sachems. . . .

"Every part of this country is sacred to my people. Every hillside, every valley, every plain and grove has been hallowed by some fond memory or some sad experience of my tribe. . . .

"The braves, mothers, glad-hearted maidens, and little children who lived here . . . still love these solitudes. Their deep fastness at eventide grows shadowy with the presence of dusty spirits. . . .

"When the last red man shall have perished from the earth and his memory among the white men shall have become a myth, these shores shall swarm with the invisible dead of my tribe. . . .

"At night when the streets of your cities and villages shall be silent, and you think them deserted, they will throng with the returning hosts that once filled and still love this beautiful land.

"The white man shall never be alone. Let him be just and deal kindly with my people, for the dead are not altogether powerless.

"Dead, did I say? There is no death, only a change of worlds."

In 1968 the Los Angeles *Herald Examiner* received so many reports of the manifestation of Native American spirits in the metropolitan area that it assigned one of its reporters, Wanda Sue Parrott, to write a special article on the phenomenon.

After describing a number of first-person accounts in her article for the "California Living" section of the newspaper, Ms. Parrott wrote that many area residents—men, women, and children alike—had shared in the ghostly Native American experience. Native American spirits had been sighted in yards, bedrooms, and living rooms at all hours of the day and night.

When one percipient found herself so unnerved by the manifestation of a Native American ghost in her home that she consulted a psychiatrist, she was told that there was nothing wrong with her; many of his patients had had similar experiences with the spirits of Native Americans.

Nearly all the witnesses agreed that the spirits were friendly and that the entities stayed for only a few moments before fading away.

In a number of cases Ms. Parrott found that the residents felt that the Native American ghosts had come to protect them or to warn them of approaching danger.

* * *

Those who follow the spiritual path of the traditional Native American Medicine priests believe in a total partnership with the world of spirits and the ability to make personal contact with individual spirit guides and those physically deceased loved ones who have already changed planes of existence.

In the traditional Native American vision quest, the seeker goes into the wilderness alone to fast, to pray, to go into the silence of meditation, and to receive a personal spirit guardian.

Don Wanatee, a Mesquakie, told me that he believed that the vision quest connects the individual with "a Higher Being who will tell you what to do and tell you the way that you must help your people, your family, and your tribe."

Silver Cloud, a Winnebago who was my personal mentor for many years in my youth, said that he fasted for twelve days and rejected all the guides who presented themselves to him until an illuminated form, composed primarily of light, appeared before him.

"You I have waited for," Silver Cloud said.

And the guide replied: "You have sought me, and you I have sought." Then it faded away.

Silver Cloud said that those who had undertaken the vision quest were required to appear before the tribal council in order to determine if the guides the young men claimed had manifested for them were genuine.

"My guide was accepted as genuine. And I don't think there is any way that any young boy could have fooled that tribal council. They knew when he had had a real experience and when he had used something as an excuse to get back to the village to get something to eat.

"One thing that we were taught is that we must *never* call upon our guides until we had exhausted every bit of physical energy and mental resource possible. Then, after we had employed every last ounce of our own reserve, we might call upon our guide, and it would appear."

While the matter of the guardian spirit may seem but a fairy tale to the ardent skeptic, as we have seen throughout the pages of this book, the concept of multidimensional beings materializing to assist humankind in times of crisis appears to be universal.

Dr. Walter Houston Clark, professor emeritus at Andover Newton Theological Seminary, once told me that upon those occasions when he had personally explored the mystical consciousness in various Native American rituals, he had assumed that any entities that he had perceived in such states were "symbols created by my unconscious, rather than coming from an intelligence in another plane of being."

Dr. Clark added, however, that he believed that "those who have received messages from cowled figures, angels, or venerable men in dreams or in visions—and then found that these messages contained verifiable truths—should treat these figures with respect, whatever their origin."

Traditional Native Americans certainly treat their guardian spirits with respect, and they use the information given to them in dreams and in visions as lessons about themselves to be used in the most effective performance of their personal medicine.

In our contemporary American society one may become rather uneasy in acknowledging a belief in a partnership with the spirit world, especially when we have learned so much about the limitless reach of the human psyche.

You might begin by at least granting the possibility that you

may establish contact with those loved ones who have gradu-
ated to other planes of existence. With a small group of like-
minded friends or family members, you could begin to sit in
development circles, remaining receptive to whatever communication might be channeled to anyone within the circle.

Under no circumstances, however, should the situation be
forced. A relaxed and tranquil state of mind will best allow the
psyche to soar free of time and space and return with images,
impressions, messages, and perhaps even a more complete
awareness of the presence of a spiritual guide.

Each session should begin with each member of the circle
praying for guidance and protection.

Once I asked Grandmother Twylah, the Repositor of Wisdom for the Seneca, how she might answer those people who
found it difficult to accept a partnership with the spirit world.
She told me, "The first thing I would say to such people is to
ask if they had ever had an experience that caused them to
wonder if there might not be a possibility of a spirit world. If
they were reluctant to discuss this, I would ask them if they
feared death.

"If they admitted such a fear, I would ask just what put
such a fear into them. Was it their religious teachings? A dread
of the unknown? In either case I would say that fear has a
great deal to do with the rejection of spirits.

"Then I might ask them if they have ever thought strongly
of a loved one who has passed over. Has it ever occurred to
them that they may have had that strong thought because that
loved one was close to them in spirit at that moment?

"I would suggest that the next time that they had such a
sensation they have a conversation with the person in spirit. I
can promise that they will have a wonderful feeling.

"Once a person opens up, the entities, the spirits, will come. Everyone wants proof of survival. So did I. I have now proved many times over the existence of the spirit world to my own satisfaction."

8. The Night I Met My Spirit Teacher

I grew up in an Iowa farm home in which we experienced continual paranormal manifestations, ranging from knockings on the wall and the sound of measured footsteps to occasional materializations, so I was rather young when I saw my first ghost.

Among my earliest childhood memories are the nocturnal visits of a somewhat stern-visaged couple who frequently walked into my bedroom at night and stood for several minutes at my bedside, looking down at me. I remember that at first I fearfully hid my head under the quilts for a few minutes, then peeped out to see if they were still there. They always were.

I soon came to understand that they meant me no harm, and although I never caught them in a smile, I had the distinct feeling that they liked me. The man wore a black suit, white shirt, and dark tie, and the woman was dressed in an old-fashioned dress with a lace collar. Years later, while paging through an old family album, I saw pictures of my great-great-grandparents Ole and Marit Christofferson Larsstuen, who had emigrated to Iowa from Norway in 1881, and I recognized them as the nocturnal visitors of my childhood.

Because of this early visitation around the age of three, coupled with a chance close encounter with a multidimensional being when I was five and my near-death experience at the age of eleven, I have been aware of the presence of unseen entities for many years. On numerous occasions throughout my life experiences a voice from some invisible entity has shouted at me to "step back" or "stay away" or "get out of here fast" and saved me from serious injury—if not death.

However, I did not actually see a Heavenly Helper face-to-face until I was in my mid-thirties.

One evening in 1972 I was awakened by some unusual sound, and I opened my eyes to see a hooded figure—like that of a cowled monk—standing at the side of my bed. In the dim light provided by an outside streetlamp, I could see that the intruder was waving his arms over me in a peculiar manner which I immediately interpreted as being threatening to the physical selves of my wife Marilyn and myself.

I was instantly wide-awake with the adrenaline pumping fiercely through my veins. I thought of my children sleeping in their bedrooms, helpless, vulnerable to attack by some vicious invader of their home and their innocence. And of course, I thought of my wife, who slept soundly, unaware of the hooded intruder in our bedroom.

I got to my knees and pulled my right arm back to deliver as solid a punch as my two hundred pounds could send straight into the face of the man who had broken into our home.

The blow never landed. I felt all of my strength draining from my body. I felt like a balloon that had suddenly lost all of its air. I had never felt so weak, so helpless in my life.

I collapsed in a heap on the mattress, and I began to cry in fear and confusion.

"Don't be afraid," the hooded intruder said in a deep male voice. "We won't hurt you."

And the next thing I knew it was morning.

I awoke with a start, my eyes desperately searching the bedroom for a hidden assailant. There was no trace of the hooded man nor any sign to prove that he had ever been there. Nothing had been taken. Nothing seemed to have been disturbed in any way.

My wife didn't have the faintest idea what I was talking about. Maybe, she suggested, it was some kind of weird dream.

Several times that day I reviewed the bizarre experience over and over in my mind. I knew that I had not been dreaming. I had definitely been awakened by an intruder who had been making some kind of strange sound.

What had he wanted?

A careful search of the house confirmed my initial assessment that nothing had been taken or disturbed in any manner whatsoever.

And mentally I kept going over the only words that he had spoken: "Don't be afraid. We [or had it been *"he"*? Had there been more than one intruder?] won't hurt you."

The next evening I was just falling asleep when I heard a peculiar, metallic buzzing sound—the kind of buzz that one would imagine a mechanical bumblebee to make. I realized at once that that must have been the strange sound that had awakened me on the night before when the cowled man had invaded our bedroom.

I lifted my head, and over my shoulder I could perceive an eerie greenish light emanating from somewhere in the stairway. Whoever it was—and perhaps by now I was beginning to think *whatever* it was—I knew that it had returned.

I felt my pulse quicken as I beheld a green globe of softly glowing light moving down the hallway toward our bedroom.

I kept telling myself over and over that I was not afraid. I was an accomplished researcher of the paranormal, and this was an excellent opportunity to study a most unusual manifestation at first hand.

Most of all, I told myself that I would definitely not—under any circumstances—*fall asleep.* On this evening's visit by the entity I would stay awake and mentally analyze every moment of the experience so that I would be able to write about it later with vivid details.

The greenish globe entered our bedroom, hovered over my face, and I heard the same deep male voice command me: "Listen!"

Once again, as on the night before, the next sensory impression that I perceived was the light of dawn entering the bedroom windows. Once again I had slept through the entire experience.

I felt terribly disgusted with myself. Why hadn't I been able to stay awake?

I have always been a night person. Since leaving teaching as a profession—along with its 7:30 A.M. classes—my average bedtime has been around 3:30 A.M. In addition to my habit of retiring at a late hour, I have always been a light sleeper, easily awakened. And once awakened, I find it difficult to return to sleep.

So how could I, of all people, not be able to stay awake when a strange hooded being and/or a peculiar green-glowing sphere entered my bedroom?

But then I began to get a different take on the whole strange business. I had awakened with the concept of a book bubbling in my brain, a book that would explore the contemporary revelatory experience. As the day progressed, I felt more and more that this idea for a new book was connected with my bedroom intruder. I also had a strong feeling that I must entitle the book *The Divine Fire.*

I called Tam Mossman, my editor at Prentice-Hall, and said that I wanted to do a book on the experiences of men and women who claim to be in spiritual communication with a Higher Intelligence. I would entitle it *Revelation: The Divine Fire.*

Tam emitted a long, low whistle and told me to go for it.

With my editor's encouragement, I set to work on the book at once, and strangely, several passages and pages of the manuscript seemed to write themselves of their own volition. I recall putting "Lucretia," my faithful old 1923 Underwood typewriter, away for the evening, probably at two or three in the morning. Then, the next thing I knew, the Dr Pepper clock on the wall was telling me that the time was now an hour or so later—and four or five pages had been added to my daily output.

I became convinced that "someone up there—or *in* there or *out* there—" had decided that this particular book had to be written—if not by me, then by some other writer or creative person.

I now began to consider my hooded bedroom invader from another perspective. Perhaps my ethereal night visitor knew very well that I have the kind of active brain that never shuts up, that never ceases an internal monologue. Whatever happens to me—good, bad, or ugly—a part of me is already working on how I will describe the experience. Just maybe my cowled friend knew that my conscious ego self had to be silenced so that my unconscious creative self could more readily receive an uninterrupted transmission from some higher level of awareness.

Shortly after the book was published by Prentice-Hall in 1973, I received a letter from a musician in the Chicago area who claimed that he had received a copy of *Revelation: The Divine Fire* in his mail *prior* to its publication. The book had arrived in a plain brown envelope with no return address or letter enclosed.

According to the musician, one night in 1972, while he was drifting off to sleep, he had received an inspiration to write a book on the contemporary revelatory experience. The title that had come to him was *The Eternal Flame.*

At the same time that I was drawing up a list of men and women to be interviewed for the book, the roster of interviewees that the musician was jotting down was almost exactly the same.

I began *The Divine Fire* with a quote from the prophet Jeremiah: "But his word was in my heart as a burning fire. . . ." For the opening words of his *The Eternal Flame,* the musician had written an original poem, which began with the line "There is a flame which burns within my heart."

Although the musician and I had received the "seed" for the book on almost exactly the same night, I was finished with my version while he was still taking research notes. The thing was, I already had the mental "writer's muscles" required to translate an inspiration for a book into the physical reality of writing a book, and I knew the exact channels to use to get the work published.

The musician, on the other hand, had been given a different set of creative "muscles," so that writing for him was a much more formidable task. When the copy of my book mysteriously manifested in his mailbox, he knew that he need not complete his work. Someone had already finished the divine assignment.

The two of us could only speculate how many other creative people were prompted by a hooded entity, an angel, a dream, or an inspiration to write a book on the contemporary revelatory experience in 1972.

To balance the cosmic scales, I should mention here that I have heard the most beautiful celestial melodies inside my head ever since I was a child—and I can't write a note of music. My newfound musician friend, on the other hand, has the "musical muscles" to translate the songs he hears in his head into notes on sheet music that others can share and enjoy.

The book *Revelation: The Divine Fire* proved to be one of the most important in my career. Reviewers were overwhelmingly responsive and thoughtful, many being generous enough to compare the work in importance with William James's *The Varieties of Religious Experience.* The book was a selection of many book clubs, including the Universe Book Club and Literary Guild, and was widely published in hardcover, quality paperback, and mass-market paperback editions.

Today, more than twenty years later, whenever Sherry and I lecture or make media-related appearances, people approach me and are kind enough to testify how that one particular book changed their lives, gave them inspiration, or provided them with strength and courage at a crisis in their lives. I, in turn, have come to feel truly privileged that I was somehow chosen to serve as the channel for the energy that the hooded being transmitted through me.

Nearly ten years later the hooded figure appeared to me again. And this time I was permitted to remain awake. On this occasion the entity presented me with the precise information that I needed to complete a very important project.

About a year later the cowled being came to me when I was truly going through a dark night of the soul. For some mysterious reason my body had become covered with painful boils and swellings. I was in a situation where I was unable to go to a medical doctor, and I lay on my bed in a miserable quandary.

When the hooded being appeared that night, he gave me

specific instructions to ingest certain combinations of foods, which I protested would likely make me feel even worse.

Rather than scold me for my ingratitude, the entity spoke soothingly and assured me that I would get well immediately if I followed his instructions.

Not able to bear even the touch of a sheet on my painful sores and boils, I was lying naked on my bed. It seemed unlikely that I would get well immediately.

That, however, is exactly what happened. I struggled to my feet, managed to mix the bizarre combination of ordinary food, ingest it—and within two or three hours all traces of the swellings had vanished from my body. And never to return, I am delighted to add.

A most important visitation from the hooded counselor and guide occurred in 1987, when he appeared in my apartment in Scottsdale, Arizona, and confirmed that Sherry Hansen was the one with whom I was to carry out the fruition of my mission on Earth.

I must emphasize that I cannot summon the hooded mentor to me whenever I wish, nor do I have any method of determining when he will manifest to me.

Although I believe that we can practice certain meditations, prayers, and attitudes that might encourage such visitations—and I will include some that I consider effective later in this book—I very much agree with those spiritual counselors who admonish us that representatives of Higher Intelligence are *sent* to us, rather than *summoned,* and that they cannot be invoked like Aladdin's genie in a bottle. To attempt to do so treads very close to Black Magic, and rather than call an angelic being to guide you, you might just be attracting an entity from the Dark Side of the Force, who will gleefully misguide you under the guise of doing your bidding.

Neither must we be drawn into any practices which may tend toward a worship of these entities. The Bible is filled with examples of angelic beings cautioning humans against bowing to them or venerating them in any manner whatsoever.

9. Pedro, the Friendly Ghost

Maurice Maeterlinck, the Belgian dramatist, essayist, and poet, once wrote his own interesting observations regarding the matter of ghosts and spirits of the dead:

> But here and there we have around us wandering intelligences, already enfranchised from the narrow and burdensome laws of space and matter, that sometimes know things that we do not know.
>
> Do they emanate from ourselves, are they manifestations of faculties as yet unknown, or are they external, objective, and independent of ourselves? Are they merely alive in the sense in which we speak of our bodies, or do they belong to bodies which have ceased to exist?
>
> . . . Once we admit their existence, which . . . is hardly contestable, it becomes less difficult to argue that they belong to the dead. . . . If experiences such as these do not demonstrate positively that the dead are able directly, demonstrably, and almost personally, to mingle with our existence and to remain in touch with us, they prove that they continue to live in us much more ardently, profoundly,

vividly, and passionately than has been hitherto
believed. . . .

When they lived outside Flagstaff, Arizona, in an old home
with a magnificently scenic view of the San Francisco Peaks,
the Stanley Fisher family had their own private ghost for four
years. "Pedro," as the coverall-clad spirit came to be called,
was a friendly spook whose presence was first revealed in
1972, when prospective son-in-law Carl Dressel stayed overnight in the upstairs guest room.

Dressel came down the next morning looking pale and
shaken.

Immediately solicitous toward their guest and likely future
family member, Betty Fisher inquired as to the cause of the
young man's apparent discomfort. She hoped that Eddie, her
three-year-old son, who was still asleep in his room, had not
fussed during the night and disturbed his rest.

"No, no, it wasn't little Eddie," Dressel assured his hostess.
"Last night I was awakened with the feeling that someone was
standing in the room watching me. I opened my eyes and saw
a heavily built man about six feet tall standing in the room."

The Fisher family sat suddenly silent over their breakfast
pancakes and scrambled eggs. Carl Dressel had their complete
attention.

"I didn't feel the man was at all hostile toward me," Dressel
explained. "He just stood there watching me. I reached over
to turn on the bed lamp, and when the light came on, the man
disappeared. I mean, he simply vanished before my eyes."

Dressel was about to say more, but Stanley Fisher inter-
rupted him: "Now let me tell you how he was dressed. He
had on some coveralls, like garage mechanics wear. He was
also wearing a plaid shirt, and his hair was kind of long."

"Daddy," nineteen-year-old Deana Fisher protested, seeking to defend her suitor, "don't be mean. Stop teasing Carl! He isn't the sort to make up things like this."

"No, really, Deana." Dressel blinked in astonishment. "Your dad is absolutely right. That's exactly how the guy was dressed!"

"But how did you know, honey?" Betty Fisher demanded of her husband. "Have you seen this mystery man prowling around our house?"

Stanley admitted that he had. "But I have concluded that he is not a man. That is, he is not a *living* man."

"Daddy!" Deana gasped. "Are you saying that we have a ghost in our house?"

"Wow!" Carl Dressel exclaimed. "A ghost! But that makes real sense all right. I'm telling you that one minute the guy was as solid as could be, then he just vanished before my eyes."

"When did you see the ghost, Stan?" Betty Fisher wanted her husband to explain.

"I first saw him about a year ago, that night when I was alone home with Eddie during that terrible thunderstorm."

Betty nodded. "The time when Deana and I had gone shopping in Phoenix and had to stay over because of all the flash flood alerts and weather warnings," she said in remembrance of the night in question.

Stanley continued: "I had just managed to get Eddie to quiet down in his bed, and I was lying on the couch in the living room with just one dim light on. After one particularly bright flash of lightning, I, too, had the feeling that someone was in the room with me.

"When I looked up, I saw a heavily built man about six feet tall, wearing a plaid sports shirt and coveralls. He at first appeared so solid that I thought that someone had broken into the house.

"Although he did not appear threatening, I yelled at him

and asked who the hell he thought he was breaking into our house.

"He gave me this kind of weird, lopsided smile, and I got off the couch and took a couple of steps toward him. As I did so, it appeared as though he took a step or two backward, then disappeared.

"I turned on the light, and he was gone. I checked all the doors and the windows, and they were all locked and undamaged.

"I didn't mention any of this at the time," Stanley Fisher confessed, "because I didn't want to upset the rest of the family."

Recently, as Stanley and Betty Fisher reminisced about the four years during which they shared their house with a ghost, they said that Stan and Carl Dressel did not long remain the only ones who had seen the friendly ghost.

"Our son, Eddie, was only about four years old that day when I scolded him for playing on the stairs," Betty said. "I told him that he must not play there, that it was dangerous.

"He looked up at me and said, 'Don't worry, Mom, I won't fall. My friend Pedro won't let me.'

"When I asked him who Pedro was, Eddie said that he was his friend who lived in his closet. Later I asked him to describe his friend, and Eddie said that Pedro wore coveralls and a bright plaid shirt.

"I felt a shiver run up my back when Eddie described his 'friend' because I was certain that we had never discussed in front of our son the ghost that Carl and Stan had seen."

As the years went by, the Fishers said that there were many additional bits of evidence to support Pedro's existence.

"Toward the end of the second year that we lived in that house, a distinct knocking sound would come from a particular section of the living-room wall each night at about eleven," Stanley Fisher said. "When we would have friends over, they, too, would be able to hear it."

One such friend was Ursula Determan of Prescott Valley, Arizona, who often visited the Fishers at their Flagstaff home.

"I definitely heard the noises," she verified. "There were these particular noises that emanated from the one living-room wall that sounded like someone or something knocking on it. The Fishers never could find the cause of it. Once when I stayed overnight with the Fishers, I had an uneasy sensation of someone being with me in the guest room."

Suspecting that any disturbance that repeated itself with such regularity had to be faulty water pipes or some other natural annoyance, Stanley Fisher tore out the wall to investigate. Workmen found nothing in the wall that could have created any kind of noise whatsoever, and the wall was rebuilt.

"As soon as the wall was refinished," Betty Fisher said, "the knockings began again, and they continued as long as we lived there."

Along with the visual materialization of the coverall-clad ghost and the nightly performance of the knockings on the living-room wall, Pedro added the sound of footsteps to his ghostly repertoire.

Deana Fisher heard the heavy footsteps on a number of occasions. "Once when I was home from college for the weekend, I kept thinking I heard someone trying to sneak up on me in my room. On another weekend, when I had a couple of girlfriends home with me, they just completely freaked out because of the sound of those ghostly footsteps. I just kept telling them that it was only Pedro, the Friendly Ghost."

One day Grandmother Fisher, who was visiting from San Diego, was treated to a wild flurry of footsteps running throughout the house. She did not think much of the sounds until it occurred to her that she was home all alone at the time.

Then, in April 1974, Pedro became a hero when a fire broke out in the house.

"According to the firemen, the blaze must have been ignited by faulty electrical wiring in the utility room," Stanley Fisher said. "We were all sound asleep in our beds when, about three-fifteen, I felt a strong hand shaking my shoulder. I woke up to see the ghostly form of Pedro standing beside our bed. I either heard him speak or I received the message telepathically: *Fire! Get up! The house is on fire!* "

Fortunately the spectrally aroused Stanley Fisher was able to get each member of the family to safety and to call the fire department in time to keep damage at a minimum.

"Pedro doesn't like the house when it is all burned," Eddie told his parents a couple of days later. "But he might come back when it is all fixed up again."

The Fishers didn't wait to see if Pedro decided to return. "I guess we took the fire as a kind of omen that was telling us to move on in our lives," Betty said. "Because of the beautiful view that our property enjoyed, we found a buyer who was willing to purchase the house on an 'as-is' basis. We moved to Albuquerque in June of 1974, and as far as we know, Pedro did not move along with us."

Stanley Fisher was quick to point out that they were very grateful to Pedro for the warning that had saved their lives. "The four of us performed a little ceremony of thanks to Pedro before we left, and we asked the Lord's blessing on him and asked that his spirit might rest in peace."

10. The Ghost of His Old Voice Teacher Sang with Him Onstage—and Still Guides Him

Ken Stevens had been nervous all evening. He was singing the lead role of the rowdy carousel barker Billy Bigelow in a Wisconsin resort's summer theater presentation of Rodgers and Hammerstein's *Carousel*, and the rumor among the cast was that there were some influential New York producers in the audience that night.

"I was about to begin singing the emotional 'If I Loved You' to the Julie Jordan character when I felt the breath go dry in my throat," Stevens recalled. "I choked back a cough—and *knew* that I could not sing another note."

He tried to swallow. He tried rolling his tongue to waken the glands in his mouth to action. He let out his breath and took in another.

Just a few more seconds and the impatient conductor would wrinkle his brow and point the baton in Stevens's direction. And instead of the confident baritone of the lusty carousel barker Billy Bigelow, Stevens could hear in his mind the rasping squawk of a summer stock amateur that would ring for months in the ears of the New York producers as the most pitiful sound that they had ever heard.

"My entire inner being cried out for help," Stevens said. 'Please, Eduardo!' I called out mentally. 'How about some help here?' "

Stevens said that his eyelids grew heavy, and he felt a calm spreading over him. "A cool draft of air enveloped me, regenerating me, reassuring me."

As though from a distance, he heard a rich baritone voice, more resonant than his own, pealing out the beautiful song that signals the awakening of love between Billy Bigelow, the coarse and shallow carousel barker, and the innocent and pure Julie Jordan. Against the painted backdrop of harbor lights, Stevens could perceive his long-dead singing teacher, Eduardo Zavala, manifesting in an ethereal form as delicate as swirling mist in the warming light of dawn. After what seemed to be a very short time later, Stevens found himself in his dressing room with no memory of having sung the rest of the performance.

"I had barely enough time to 'wake up' when my dressing room was filled with people congratulating me on an emotionally moving performance," he said. "A couple of the New York producers liked my interpretation of Billy Bigelow so much that they offered me the role of Don Quixote in a touring company of *Man of La Mancha*."

Stevens, who now teaches theater production in a college in the Pacific Northwest, attended one of our seminars in Portland, Oregon, and over coffee in the hotel restaurant, he told Sherry and me about his consistent help from the spirit world.

"Eduardo was there for me time after time in theaters and concert halls all over North America," he said. "He had been my singing teacher back in New Jersey when I was a kid. He was always so generous in his praise of my talent, and he promised that he would always be there when I needed him.

"I was devastated when he was killed in a train-car accident when I was nineteen, but his spirit appeared to me not long after his funeral and told me that he would still keep his promise always to be with me."

All this seemed quite normal and natural for young Ken Stevens, for, he told us, his grandmother Natasha was well known as a spirit medium in the old neighborhood back in New Jersey.

"My mom was also heavy into Spiritualism, and my dad was tolerant of her beliefs," Stevens said. "I grew up hearing the sound of spirit rappings on our walls, and I was amazed to hear the various voices from beyond the veil of death speaking through the throat of Grandma Natasha."

When she did a spirit reading for Ken when he was eleven, Grandma Natasha had told him that he could be successful as a singer, a teacher, or an army officer. He chose to follow his first love of singing, knowing that the great Eduardo Zavala lived in their neighborhood. Since the former opera singer was a friend of the family's and a client of Grandma Natasha's, young Ken was certain that he would agree to be his teacher.

Zavala made the youngster understand that training the voice was a long and arduous process, especially for one who planned to sing professionally. There was the everlasting need to maintain superior posture; there were the breathing exercises so that depth and ease of air intake might be controlled. At the same time one must learn to keep the neck and upper chest relaxed.

"During those years of intense study," Ken Stevens told us, "Eduardo Zavala and I developed a love and rapport between us that death could not break. I would have to say that I believe Eduardo to be my spirit guide.

"I don't really consider myself a Spiritualist in the sense that

my mother and grandmother are, but I have observed so
many genuine phenomena in my life that I know that one can
learn a great deal about the true nature of humankind through
a study of these kinds of manifestations.

"But as I said, without equivocation I believe that Eduardo
is my spirit guide. I often feel his presence with me, and I
know that I can call upon him whenever I need his special
kind of assistance. I don't sing professionally too much any-
more, but I feel that his guidance helps me to be a better
teacher of young people. And he has warned me a number of
times to remove myself from potential danger."

This seems to be an appropriate place to draw a distinction
between the mystical or supernormal guidance that comes
from angelic intelligence and that which comes from a spirit
guide.

Paul V. Johnson, director of the Spiritual Advisory Council
in Summerfield, Florida, explains that angels differ in kind
from discarnate spirits. "Angels have never lived in a physical
body, so the energy interaction is of a different vibration and
does not carry with it limitations acquirable in physical incar-
nations.

"With proper alignment, all spiritual guidance has a positive
potential benefit if we seek it and are willing to take respon-
sibility for it. When we are truly ready, guidance arrives and of
the kind needed at that particular time. Integrity is an essential
ingredient of spirituality."

11. Father McQuire's Personal Guardian Angel

When I first heard Father Pat McQuire tell this story, he was in his mid-seventies. Although he often recounted the tale, the details never varied, and I understood perfectly why the story meant so much to him. In a very real sense it provided him with all the proof that he ever needed that his faith in God was capable of producing miracles and manifesting a ministering angel to watch over him.

Father McQuire was just a young man, not yet thirty, when, in 1923, he was sent by his church to minister to a parish in a tough mining town in West Virginia.

"I hadn't been there long in my new assignment when I was called to visit a man who was dying," the priest said. "Although I was very new to the area, I knew that this particular address was a little out in the country, and because I had no car at that time, I would have to walk quite a distance down a dark and lonely road. I don't mind admitting that I was a bit nervous."

When the young priest finally reached the address, he found that there was no one ill there at all. "The door was opened by a coarse man who reeked of cheap whiskey and who cursed me for disturbing his sleep."

Certain that he had written down the correct address and that he had not made a mistake, a puzzled Father McQuire set out on the walk back to the church.

"As I trudged down that darkened road, I kept praying for protection," he said. "I could only conclude that I had been the butt of someone's senseless and cruel joke. I hoped that while I was off on that wild-goose chase, someone who really needed me hadn't called."

The years passed. What the young priest had hoped would be only a temporary assignment had grown into nearly thirty years of service to the parish in the rowdy mining town. But in the meantime, Father McQuire had come to love and respect the integrity and the dignity that the greater number of his parishioners maintained throughout the course of their difficult struggle to survive their often mean existence in the mines.

"I had been in the community going on thirty years when I received a call from the state prison that a man on death row had asked to see me," Father McQuire said.

"I did not know the man and had never met him, but when the warden repeated the name a few times, I remembered reading some years back about the terrible murders that the man had committed while robbing a small family-owned restaurant."

Father McQuire traveled to the prison, wondering all during the drive why this particular individual wished to see him.

The inmate of death row was quick to ask the priest to hear his confession.

"Certainly," Father McQuire agreed. "But there is a Roman

Catholic chaplain who serves this prison. Why did you summon me from such a distance to hear your confession?"

"Because I know that you are a special kind of priest," the
convict answered.

Father McQuire laughed. "There's nothing special about
me, my son. I'm a poor priest serving a poor parish in a small
mining town."

"Oh, I know exactly who you are, Father. Do you remember answering a false alarm about a dying man right after you
got in town in 1923?"

Father McQuire was taken quite by surprise. "Why, yes,
nearly thirty years ago. I had nearly forgotten. Though I don't
know how I could ever forget walking down that dark and
scary road."

"I was the one who sent you the phony message."

"You? But why?"

The murderer paused to grind out his cigarette beneath his
heel. "I was a tough eighteen-year-old punk, and I wanted to
lure you out there on that dark road so I could rob you."

"Rob me?" Father McQuire felt momentarily foolish for
playing the role of an echo, but he was stunned by the convict's confession. "I didn't have two nickels to rub together."

The prisoner nodded. "Yeah, maybe. But the word was that
you had just come from Chicago and that you were rich. Word
was that you always carried a good-sized roll with you."

Father McQuire shook his head in disbelief. "So then why
didn't you rob me? I certainly was vulnerable all alone out
there on that dark and lonely road."

"I intended to," the man said in a soft, measured voice. "I
had been laying in wait in these bushes for hours, waiting for
you to show. Then, when you did, you had this big bruiser
walking alongside you."

"What big bruiser? I was alone. I didn't even see anyone
else on the road."

"He was walking with his hand on your shoulder, like he was your bodyguard ready to protect you."

Father McQuire's mouth opened and closed a couple of times, but no words were ready to come out.

"I watched the two of you walk away from me," the convict said, "and I was crying to myself about losing all that dough that people said you carried with you.

"And then, just when you are about out of my sight, I see this big lug with his arm around your shoulder just disappear. I mean, he vanished into nothing. And then I realized that you had your own special guardian angel.

"That's why I never messed with you again, and that's why I want you to hear my confession before the warden turns out my lights for good. And I know I ain't gonna be with any angels where I'm going!"

It would usually be at this point that Father McQuire would tamp the tobacco in the bowl of his brier pipe and conclude the story with a blessing for his listeners: "So that's the story of my own personal guardian angel, and may the good Lord see to it that yours is as big and burly a lad as my own."

12. A Dead Neighbor's Spirit Rescued Them from a Fiery Death

The British novelist William Makepeace Thackeray presented a ready answer to all skeptics of ghostly phenomena when he said, "It is all very well for you who have never seen a ghost to talk as you do; but had you seen what I have witnessed, you would hold a different opinion."

In May 1990 the ghost of their dead neighbor saved Cindy Johnson and her family from a possible death by fire or smoke inhalation.

"At that time I lived with my husband, Ernie, and our three kids in a fourplex apartment in Charlotte, North Carolina," Cindy said. "That winter our neighbor Marla, a sickly young woman in her early twenties, had been suffering with advanced stages of leukemia. Marla had been such a cheerful, hardworking lady that it was hard on all of us who were her friends to see her becoming so ill and suffering in so much pain."

When Marla's steady boyfriend stopped coming around to

see her, Cindy tried to take even more time from her busy schedule to spend with her.

"It was hard to get away from my own duties, what with three little kids and all, but Marla had always been there to help me with baby-sitting and other things whenever she could, so I wanted to offer some kind of support for her in her hour of need. I usually had to wait until Ernie was home from work because I didn't want any of our babies saying anything hurtful to Marla. You know, like why did she look so awful and stuff like that."

Marla died in April. "She was courageous and cheerful to the very end," Cindy said. "I so admired her spirit, and all of us in the fourplex considered it a real tragedy that such a good person had to die so young."

One night, about a month after Marla's passing, Cindy was in bed with her husband, just starting to drift off to sleep. "I had been feeling kind of restless," Cindy said. "You know, worry about bills and stuff, and if Matissa, our daughter, was going to have to have braces on her front teeth.

"Anyway, as I was finally falling asleep, I rolled over on my side, and there, solid as life, standing right by my side of the bed, was Marla.

"I wasn't scared of her being a ghost and all, but I admit that I was startled to see her there."

Cindy blinked her eyes and shook her head. When the image of Marla remained at her bedside, she giggled and said, "I always thought that if I ever saw a ghost, I would be scared silly. But I'm not at all afraid of you, Marla."

Marla's spirit form smiled, but her features immediately became very serious in appearance. "Girl, if you don't get up and get your family out of here, you're gonna be a ghost just like me!"

With that warning pronounced, Marla's image vanished.

"But she surely had my complete attention," Cindy said. "I

wasn't ready to be a ghost yet. I had three little kids to get raised."

Cindy elbowed her husband into reluctant wakefulness. "Ernie, I just saw Marla's ghost, and she told me that we have to get out of the house."

Ernie rubbed his eyes, glanced wearily at the bedside clock. "It's two o'clock. What are you doing waking me up at this hour? You know I've got to be at work by six. I need my sleep."

"But I saw Marla's ghost, and she told me to get us up and out of here," Cindy argued.

"You're crazy, woman," Ernie grumbled. "You just had a dream about her. Now let me get back to sleep, and you do the same."

After a few more minutes of arguing about the reality of Marla's ghost and the urgency of her warning, Cindy finally convinced Ernie to get out of bed and at least look around the fourplex.

"Hey," Ernie said as he shoved his feet into his slippers at the side of the bed, "am I smelling smoke?"

Suddenly wide-awake, Ernie ran to the door of their apartment and opened it to find the hallway beginning to fill with thin tendrils of smoke.

"My God," he shouted back to Cindy, "the place must be on fire! You get the kids up and dial nine-one-one, and I'll wake the others in the building!"

Within minutes the Johnson family had vacated their apartment and had spread the alarm that saved the other lives in the fourplex.

Because of the early detection of the fire, the firemen were able to keep damage to a minimum. It was revealed that the new occupant in Marla's old apartment, a heavy cigarette smoker, had accidentally dropped a live butt in the cushions of an easy chair before he had gone out to shop at an all-night supermarket.

In the days that followed, Cindy said that she was not at all shy about letting everyone know that they all owed their continued existence on the Earthplane to the warning message of Marla's ghost.

13. An Angel Delivered Her Father from a Terrible Curse

"Magic is our will to live," Beatrice Gompu said one afternoon as we had coffee in the college cafeteria after class. "We Africans look back now and stand amazed at the resources of our forefathers. They followed all kinds of occupations in search of power, security, and health. Magic was one of them."

A lovely and graceful young woman from Uganda, Beatrice and I became good friends when she enrolled in the creative writing class that I taught in a small midwestern college. Her father was a very wealthy man in her hometown in Uganda, and because she was the favorite child of her father's favorite wife, she had been allowed to travel to the United States to further her education. Her actual birth name was Mone, but she had acquired the name of Beatrice so she might be numbered among the Christian children and be allowed to go to a Christian school.

"Magic is completely integrated into all aspects of our life in my region of Uganda," she continued. "Magic is always there with us—alive, invigorating, but often very deadly.

"For instance, I found that the only thing that could stop

the evil magic of a terrible curse that had been set against my father was my prayers to the angels of light," she told me and a couple of the other students from class who had now joined us at a quiet booth in a corner of the cafeteria.

"On some level of knowing I felt that these angels had always been with me—long before the missionaries told me about them. Perhaps in Africa we equate them more often with nature spirits, devas, as I have heard some Hindu students call them. I believe that the word 'deva' is from the Sanskrit for 'radiant being.' "

When I agreed with her identification of the devic entities, I urged her to tell us the story of how angels had been able to rescue her father from a curse that had been set against him. It was obvious that the others from the writing class were also very interested in hearing another of Beatrice's captivating tales of Africa.

It seemed that Beatrice's father, Martin Gompu, had been ill for a long time, and no practitioner of Western medicine in the region was able to determine the exact nature of his illness. Their village witch doctor had pronounced the sickness a very strange one and frankly admitted his inability to effect a cure.

Her father had always been a stubborn man, wild, strong, defiant, proud, and prosperous. It was natural that such a man should acquire enemies. The green-eyed monster of jealousy had prompted more than one business competitor to gaze with envy at the wealthy man with eight daughters, whose prospective sons-in-law would steadily assure him of even more wealth.

"But Saja was the only jackal who had become jealous enough to try to kill my father," Beatrice said. "He was a weak little man who was Father's principal rival in the village. And now it seemed that he had brooded upon Father's rise to prosperity until he could no longer sit passively by and let the fortunate man acquire more property and more possessions.

"Saja knew that he was far too puny and weak to fight my big, strong father physically, so he had sought out the most powerful witch doctor in the area and paid him to cast a dread curse upon him."

The curse had proved to be most effective. Beatrice told us that her father waged a ceaseless war against his unknown illness for nearly six years. If it had not been for his great physical strength, he surely would have died as he went from witch doctor to mission doctor to witch doctor in a vain attempt to find relief from his awful malady.

"At last Father was able to locate a witch doctor whose skill in magic was even more accomplished than the one that Saja had paid to curse him," Beatrice said, "and he was cured."

Many times after her father's recovery Beatrice heard Saja swearing and fulminating at him whenever the two of them met in the marketplace. Throughout all his afflictions she never once heard her father curse Saja or vow vengeance on the evil little merchant.

Beatrice also found it very ironic that Saja's nephew and only male heir, Amisi, was her brother John's best friend.

"I had also felt that Amisi, the little snake, was only trying to ingratiate himself to my family because he was aware that one day he and John would be the two central figures in the village, and his greedy mind envisioned a coalition between the two most powerful families," Beatrice said.

Beatrice was always appalled by the seemingly endless parameters of Amisi's greed. "Often he would bring baskets of fruits as gifts to our family—and then he would proceed to eat every piece of the fruit during the course of his evening visit."

The sinister Saja had not taken at all well to his being

thwarted in his attempt to hex his chief competitor, Martin Gompu. After an extensive search of the outlying villages, he managed to find a witch doctor whose death-dealing curses were as feared by the native people as much as early inhabitants of our American West might have feared the deadly six-gun prowess of a professional gunfighter.

"Our father's terrible ordeal reached its climax one stormy night—a night of thunder, wind, and lightning, a night made for the working of Black Magic," Beatrice said.

"Father had been gone for several days on a long business trip. On this night of the violent storm we suddenly heard chanting outside our home. When we looked out the windows, we were astonished to see Saja and a fierce-looking witch doctor standing outside in the stormy darkness. A small crowd of men had gathered around them to watch the ensuing drama."

"This time I have you, Martin Gompu!" Saja's cackle sounded about the noise of the storm. "This time, my prosperous friend, you shall die!"

"If you fail this time, Saja," a voice mocked at him from the crowd, "you are not a man."

"I shall not fail!" Saja shouted at his unseen accuser. "No one can match the might of my witch doctor's magic!"

With shocked, incredulous eyes, Beatrice's family watched helplessly as Saja and his master witch doctor performed the dark rites necessary to bring about the destruction of their husband, father, and head of the household.

A young goat was led into the magic circle by one of Saja's servants, and the witch doctor raised his angry features to the night rain, his lips mouthing curses, his red, devilish eyes burning beneath his protruding forehead and feathered headdress.

"There can be no escape for Martin Gompu," the witch

doctor proclaimed to all within the sound of his harsh, croaking voice. "He will die in disgrace away from his home, and the curse will remain upon his family."

Beatrice told us that she would never forget the way the witch doctor looked at them when he pronounced those hateful words. "The worm Amisi stood on the other side of the fence, and his pitiful expression seemed to plead with us to understand that he was helpless to come to our aid."

She confessed that she had screamed when the witch doctor slit the goat's throat.

"Everyone knew that as soon as the goat was killed in sacrifice, something horrible would happen to my father," Beatrice said.

"The goat lay kicking, its blood spurting from its throat. The witch doctor beckoned, and Saja began jumping with his bare feet into the spilled blood of the goat. After he had performed his part in the ritual, each member of his family was made to observe the same blood curse against my family and all of our family."

That was when Beatrice began to pray the hardest. "I asked all those angels of light who were in the Bible and who the missionaries said were still all around us, watching over us, protecting us, to stand guard over my father. As I said before, somehow I felt within my very soul that I had known the presence of those guardian spirits before in my life, and I asked them please to manifest to protect my father on his homeward journey."

The witch doctor tossed the carcass of the goat on the sacrificial fire that had been built, and as he turned to leave, he made his final pronouncement of the terrible evening of storm and evil. "No one is to touch the goat meat," he said to the assembled crowd of onlookers and the members of Saja's family. "If any of you do so, the curse will be yours!"

Beatrice and her family, enveloped in grief and horror, huddled in their home. The ceremony had begun a few minutes before nine. The witch doctor had slit the goat's throat and directed the curse at her father at exactly nine o'clock. It was now ten. Their father—if he was unharmed—should arrive home at any minute.

Soon it was eleven o'clock. In terror the family of Martin Gompu watched the inexorable movement of the hands of the clock.

When midnight had passed, they retained their silent, prayerful vigil—but they had begun to fear the worst.

It was two forty-five when they heard the sputtering of Odembo, the family automobile. Of all the men who had gone on the business trip, only Beatrice's father could drive a car. That meant that he was alive!

"Father and his companions were a physical mess," Beatrice remembered with a broad smile. "They were soaked, splattered with mud, and completely exhausted—but they were still alive."

As his family hugged and kissed him, Martin Gompu explained that a strange thing had occurred as they approached the main bridge over the river. A man with a lantern had jumped in front of the car with his arms outstretched, as if warning them.

When he applied the breaks of Odembo to miss hitting the man in the road, the car had slid into the ditch.

"When we got out of the car, the man with the lantern was nowhere to be seen," Beatrice's father said. "It was as if he had disappeared."

Beatrice knew with a quickening of her heart that the stranger with the lantern had been an angel manifesting in answer to her prayer.

"While the rest of us were pushing the car out of the ditch, one of the fellows walked on ahead on toward the bridge." Martin Gompu continued his account. "He discovered that the rickety old wooden bridge had been struck by lightning from the storm and had collapsed into the river.

"If we had continued on, we would have slid into the rushing water—instead of the ditch—and probably have drowned. That fellow with the lantern had warned us and saved our lives.

"With the bridge out, we had to take the long way home. That's what took us so long."

"What time was that, Father?" Beatrice asked. "What time was it that you saw the man with the lantern and Odembo slid into the ditch?"

Her father shrugged, frowned, then smiled. "Yes, I remember looking at my wristwatch just before the man appeared on the road. It was exactly nine o'clock."

"That was the very moment that Saja's new witch doctor, a master of the dark forces, slit the goat's throat in front of our house and sent a death curse flying toward you, Father," Beatrice told him.

It seemed that she was the only member of the family who was able to find her tongue and explain the significance of the fortuitous accident to the bewildered man, who could only stare in amazement at his weeping family as they gathered around him.

"My prayer to the angels of light had been answered," Beatrice said, concluding her remarkable story. "A holy being bearing a lantern appeared on the road and prevented my father and his friends from drowning in the river.

"But the heavenly guardians performed a twist on the acts of the evildoers that I never would have thought of," she told us.

"His family found Amisi the next morning quite dead. In his

mouth was a piece of goat meat. He just could not resist having at least one little bite of the sacrificial animal. By his so doing, his insatiable greed had transferred the effects of the witch doctor's curse from my father to him and his family."

14. Reading the Palm of a Benevolent Spirit Being

A few years ago I learned of a very interesting "ghost" photograph that had been taken by a woman in a small town in southern Minnesota. She seemed embarrassed when I called upon her and she learned that I had somehow found out about the strange photo. She had absolutely no interest in the paranormal, in attempted communication with the Other Side, or in calling any special attention to herself.

I quickly ascertained that the house in which the visitation had occurred was a new one. It was not a creaking old manse with a history of hauntings. It was not a home in which people had died either naturally or unnaturally.

In other words, there was no clue in the immediate environment of the house that would have given any indication of the actual identity of a man or a woman who might have felt drawn to the place after his or her transition to another realm of existence.

According to the percipient—the woman who had witnessed the manifestations—she had first seen the ghostly image of a human hand in her home during the Christmas season of the previous year. She would be putting on makeup, and she would see the phantom fingers reflected behind her. She would perceive a slight feeling of unease while working in the kitchen, whirl about, and catch a glimpse of the ghostly hand hovering just a few feet behind her.

The thing had at last faded from view and was not seen again for the rest of the year—until the Christmas just past.

On Christmas Eve, while she was in the process of snapping a picture of her husband assembling a farm set for Santa's morning visit to the children, her attention was drawn to the television set—which had been unplugged and moved from its usual place to make room for the Christmas tree. There she once again clearly saw the image of an outstretched hand facing her.

She began to move the camera lens to focus on the mysterious hand and to take its picture to prove the truth of her once-a-year Christmas ghost sightings, but before she could snap the photograph, the image faded away. If only, she sighed to her astonished husband, she had noticed the ghostly image in time to have obtained photographic evidence of the thing's occasional existence.

It was not until the following May, when she decided at last to share an account of the ghost hand's existence with a group of friends, that someone suggested that she might have captured the image of the spectral holiday visitor unknowingly while she had been concentrating on taking the surprise photograph of her husband.

As is the case in so many families, pictures are taken to commemorate holidays, birthdays, and anniversaries and the film remains in the camera until all the exposures have been gradually used up.

Intrigued by her friend's suggestion, she quickly exposed

the remaining pictures on the roll and sent the film away to be processed.

When the prints were returned, she discovered that she almost certainly *had* caught the ghostly image of the mystery hand on film. There, hovering just in front of the television set, was the clear image of an open outstretched hand in the classic "helping hand" posture.

Once again she reminded me that the television set had been *unplugged,* an assertion that is verified by the photograph since a section of cord with the plug visible is easily seen on the floor near the set. The hand, then, is definitely not a flickering televised impression made stationary by what would have to have been the accidental timing of her simple Instamatic's factory-set lens.

Since the lines in the palm of the mysterious hand were quite well formed and reasonably clear, it occurred to me to send an enlargement of the photograph to Marge Tellez, an accomplished palmist in Sacramento, California. Here, somewhat condensed and abridged, is Marge's most interesting analysis of the palm of a citizen from an invisible world:

Head Line: When a Head Line goes the full width of the palm, such as in this entity's case, it indicates one whose mind works very fast.

This being's Head Line slopes ever so slightly into Luna, showing one who has creative abilities and an imagination that is under control.

Heart Line: The entity's Heart Line starts in the Jupiter Mount, thus indicating someone who idealizes those he or she loves.

Fate Line: There seems to be a line coming from the Mount of Luna, which would suggest a person who has been active in working with the public in some way.

There is a branch line running toward Jupiter, which indicates success.

Line of Brilliancy: Coming from Luna, as this line does, it reveals someone who has enjoyed a brilliant, successful occupation—one in which creative and imaginative talents would be utilized.

Girdle of Venus: This being's Girdle of Venus indicates a person who is very sensitive.

In fact, this entity possesses such a vivid, creative mind that he/she can picture anything with great reality. This person can project life into things and cause them to come alive.

The Thumb: Even though it is quite long, it is well balanced, indicating a very strong-willed person.

First Phalange: This also suggests an entity with a very strong will.

Second Phalange: This is a being who uses logic in all things.

Third Phalange (Mount of Venus): Because it is so exceptionally well developed, it indicates one who relates well to others, who permits the free flow of emotions.

Set of the Thumb: This reveals one who has much compassion for others.

Set of the Fingers: How the fingers are set on the palm shows a very well-balanced individual.

Jupiter (First Finger): The extreme length of this being's First Finger reveals great leadership ability and a strength of personality.

Saturn (Second Finger): The length of this finger indicates an individual who is not afraid to take chances to achieve worthwhile goals.

Mercury (Fourth Finger): The shortness of this finger reveals a lack of sexual involvement. It reveals an entity that is celibate or perhaps asexual in nature.

What kind of entity—according to the analysis of a widely known professional palmist—was the owner of the mysterious hand that materialized on two consecutive Christmas holidays in a Minnesota home?

The being was possessed of an alert, logical mind and exercised great powers of creativity.

The entity was a strong-willed, loving, compassionate individual who had established a balance between the physical and the spiritual.

Finally, the being lived a celibate, perhaps asexual existence.

It would seem to me that such qualities as a powerful, creative mind and a loving, compassionate nature, as well as balanced emotions and an asexual existence, might be said to describe very well the attributes that I would suppose an angel to possess. And if not an angel, then a spirit that had risen to higher dimensions of reality and maintained a benevolent interest in us mortals here on Earth.

Interestingly, after its picture was taken, the hand never again appeared in the home. The normal, average midwestern family went about its normal, average tasks without any further paranormal disruptions of its established and comfortable schedule of activities.

* * *

Why did the hand appear?

On the snapshot it is poised forever as if representing a "helping hand," a symbol that there is an eternally powerful energy source from which any man or woman might seek power and inspiration—a symbol, to put it another way, that none of us ever truly walks alone.

Why did it appear in this family's home? Did they need such assurance?

Perhaps.

Or maybe, once it was frozen in time by the synchronous snapping of a simple camera lens, it will forever be able to serve as a reassuring symbol of loving, angelic companionship to all those who see the photograph.

15. The Spirit of a Dead Professor Helped Them Pass Their Math Exam

Randall Egland of Arlington Heights, Illinois, wrote to request one of our questionnaires on paranormal experiences and to tell us of a ghostly encounter that had enabled him to pass a crucial math examination when he was a student at a midwestern college in 1986.

"My girlfriend, Lisa Estrada, and I were up really late one night cramming for a very important math exam in the spring term," Egland said. "We were both juniors who had discovered that we lacked a specific credit in mathematics which the college required for graduation. There was an obvious reason why we both lacked this credit: We both hated math with a passion.

"For students such as ourselves, the college thoughtfully provided a course entitled Basic Principles of Mathematics, which, among the students, was known unflatteringly as Bonehead Math. As embarrassing as it is to admit, even this course was giving us major stress."

Randall Egland remembered clearly that it was almost the

very stroke of three o'clock in the morning when the supernatural incident occurred.

"We were seated in an area that was surrounded by darkness. The only illumination came from the desk lamp over our
study table.

"I was about to hang it up. I rationalized to Lisa that since
we were both better-than-average students in our other
courses, maybe we should stop trying to cram, get some sleep
before the test, do the best we could—which we both knew
would be terrible—and if we failed the test and got a D for the
course, perhaps our other grades would balance things out on
our grade point average.

"It was at just that point that a voice from out of the darkness said, 'My dear young man, please don't give up so easily.' "

Lisa could not suppress a small scream of surprise, and
Egland admitted that assuming that they were alone in the
darkened study area, he, too, had been startled by the voice.

"Then this little old man with a shaggy mane of snow white
hair stepped out of the shadows. He was dressed in a dark
suit with a white shirt and a floppy polka-dotted bow tie, and
he came walking straight to our study table and asked us what
we were doing up so late.

"When we told him that we were doing our best not to
flunk a big math test the next day, he smiled and introduced
himself as Professor Martin, who had taught in the mathematics department for many years.

"When Lisa said that she had never seen him around the
campus, he quickly explained that he was now retired, a professor emeritus."

Before they were barely finished with introductions, the
kindly old professor asked if he might be of assistance to them
by explaining some of the math problems with which they
were struggling.

"Professor Martin really had a gift for making the complicated seem simple," Egland said. "He was a fantastic teacher. We couldn't help expressing our inner thoughts that we wished that he were our teacher in Bonehead Math."

Professor Martin laughed heartily. "Do they still call it that? Bonehead Math. I think I first heard a student use that colorfully apt derogatory term in 1943. Well, believe me, young people, I, too, wish that I were still teaching in these beloved old halls of ivy."

When Randall and Lisa left the study area at around five in the morning, they both thanked Professor Martin heartily and complimented him with the truthful acknowledgment that they had never before so clearly understood the essentials of mathematics. Since the exam was at eight-thirty, they decided to forget about sleep and to have some coffee and breakfast before class.

"We both passed the test with grades beyond our expectations," Egland wrote. "Later that day, after we had each made it through our last class of the afternoon, Lisa and I decided to stop by the administration building and get Professor Martin's address. We wanted to send him a nice thank-you note for his kindness in providing us with an impromptu math tutoring session."

The two students were startled when an officious young secretary informed them that Professor Richard Alan Martin had died in 1963.

"But that's impossible," Lisa protested. "We were with him until nearly dawn this morning."

The secretary looked up at Lisa and smiled. "Not unless you can communicate with the dead, you weren't. Our records show that Professor Martin retired from full-time teaching in 1950, taught part-time until 1958, and died in 1963 at the age of eighty-three. You have to be mistaken. It must have been someone else."

Egland and Lisa asked if they might see a picture of Professor Martin in a college yearbook of that vintage.

"Although the secretary was becoming quite impatient with us at this point, she complied with our request," Randall Egland wrote in his report of the experience.

"When she returned a few minutes later with a 1958 yearbook, Lisa and I got shivers of recognition when we turned to the page with Professor Martin's faculty photograph. There was no question in either of our minds that he was the kindly gentleman who had tutored us so patiently."

A few days later, after their next math class, Egland and Lisa stayed after class in order to ask their instructor, Professor Gehling, if he had ever known Professor Richard Alan Martin.

"Why, yes." He smiled broadly. "Why do you ask? Has his ghost been popping up again in the dormitory study areas?"

When both Lisa and Egland were caught off guard by Professor Gehling's direct question of a campus haunting, he took their stunned silence as a negative response. "Well, it's probably just a silly college tradition," he explained, "but for several years after his death a number of students claimed to have seen his ghost walking about. I'm sorry. I didn't mean to seem rude by answering your question in such a dramatic way."

"Then you did know Professor Martin?" Lisa prompted.

"Oh, very well, indeed," Professor Gehling replied. "In fact, I had him for an instructor when I was an undergraduate student from 1949 to 1952. He was my inspiration, perhaps the best teacher I ever had. And he was never reluctant to show his students that he truly cared about their well-being even more than he cared about their ability to comprehend mathematics. I have always hoped that I might be even half as effective a teacher as he was."

As they left the classroom, Egland recalled that both he and Lisa had felt a "warm glow inside, just considering the fact that Professor Richard Alan Martin, who so loved his students while he was alive, could still materialize on occasion to guide them after his death."

16. The Gentle Ghost Forwarded a Letter from Beyond to Prove Its Existence

This case was unique in so many interesting ways, not the least of which was the arrival of a letter that had apparently been in limbo for more than forty years. It is always exciting when a ghost provides physical proof of its existence.

The flower children in the commune in the middle-size city in Illinois had got in touch with me through a friend, a radio talk host on whose program I used to appear quite frequently. It seems that they were being frightened out of their wits by the manifestation of a ghost, and they wondered if I might arrange to pay a visit to their abode in the company of a professional psychic-sensitive of good reputation and check out the cosmic disturbances.

Since my schedule permitted such an expedition during that very warm July in 1970, I arranged to have a top-notch medium—I'll call her Phyllis—fly into the Illinois city and meet me at my friend's radio station, from which point we would enlist him to drive us to the commune in question.

"I've come to know these kids a bit since I first called you, Brad," Matt said as he drove us to the house. "I've gone to the commune and visited with them a couple of times. They're not at all a bad bunch. In fact, the fellow most troubled by the haunting is really quite a talented artist, and they are all eager to see if Phyllis can find out what's been going on in their commune."

The house was classic midwestern Victorian, probably built sometime in the 1890s. According to Matt, the young hippies had persuaded the current owner not to tear the place down but to allow them to rent it for a minimal fee in return for their restoring the home to its former glory. I did not wish to express negative "vibes," but I could not help observing that the run-down outward appearance of the house indicated that they had a long way to go.

In answer to our knock at the front door, two young men with shoulder-length hair stepped out on the front porch, flashed us the peace sign, and smiled a welcome. Their bib overalls were colorfully stitched with multicolored patches. One young man was barefoot; the other wore heavy work shoes that he had painted a bright red.

Melville, our principal host, was a tall, thin man with long hair, a full beard, and the red work shoes. A shorter fellow, with a name something like Peapod, was never far from his side. Melville's wife, Shanti, was a quiet, deeply tanned, lovely young woman whose bare feet and rainbow-colored toenails peeped out at us from beneath what appeared to be a long, tie-dyed nightshirt. During the course of our investigations we nodded our greetings to a number of smiling, mellowed-out young people with colorful, individualized costumes, who sat at leisure in various downstairs rooms, but few of them contributed anything of real value to our work.

Within a few moments of our arrival and after all the proper introductions had been exchanged, Phyllis told Shanti that psychically she had heard her calling, "Charlie, Charlie, Charlie," as Matt was driving us to the house.

"Oh, wow." The young woman laughed. "Charlie is my cat. She had her kittens yesterday, and I couldn't find them outside. I was calling her just a few minutes before you arrived."

"Schiller," Phyllis said, looking directly at Melville. "I hear the name Schiller around you. He's a minister or a priest. He's a bit taller than you. You stood in the rain and talked to him outside a church . . . two . . . maybe three nights ago."

"Weird stuff, lady." Melville shook his head. "I'm going to be best man at a friend's wedding next weekend. A couple of nights ago I stood in the rain outside Pastor Schiller's church, and we talked about the ceremony."

Phyllis smiled triumphantly. I knew that she was just showing off a bit for the young people. Also, such a display of her psychic prowess served at once to break the ice and to convince strangers that she was indeed the real thing.

A few moments later we found ourselves in a stuffy upstairs room where an entity had once chased Melville and Shanti and given them a good scare.

The room was bare of all furniture except for an old wooden dresser painted with stars and stripes that sat lonely and little used in a far corner. Someone's bedroll lay sprawled beneath an open window. A large painting of a sad-eyed unicorn bound with ropes and chains dominated an entire wall.

"We were listening to records up here when the thing materialized. It just didn't seem to want us in here," Melville explained.

Phyllis seemed to be sniffing the air long after the physical fact. "You were burning incense and sitting around the record player by candlelight. And someone . . . whoever . . . sat over there against the wall . . . pounding some weird little drums."

Shanti smiled, nodded her head. "Yes, we were sitting around like that. And my brother, Ray, from Madison was playing the bongos."

"And you were all eating slices of watermelon," Phyllis continued. "And drinking wine."

"Cool." Melville laughed in approval of the psychic's accuracy. "Right on."

"And you were smoking long pipes," Phyllis added.

Melville lost his broad smile and began to study the tips of his red work shoes.

"What was in those pipes, guys?" Matt asked with a chuckle. "Sir Walter Raleigh tobacco, no doubt."

"Was that when the apparition appeared?" Phyllis wanted to know. "Right after you started smoking grass?"

Shanti cleared her throat to prompt a response to the question.

"I guess it was," Melville admitted.

Shanti stamped one of her bare feet in an impatient little drumbeat and crossed her arms across her chest. "I tried to tell you guys that grass can stir up spirits, didn't I? But would you listen. Oh, no, what do *I* know?"

"I think this entity was somehow offended by marijuana being smoked in her bedroom," Phyllis said.

"*Whose* bedroom? What *her*?" Peapod or whoever spoke up for the first time since his mumbled introduction of himself downstairs.

"I'm picking up the image of a kind, gentle woman," Phyllis said. "Someone who used to live here. Someone who loved this house. Someone who was very, well, what you might call prim and proper."

Melville grinned awkwardly. "Oh, wow, prim and proper. She must go bananas in this house now."

"Why is that?" Matt couldn't help teasing. "You fine young folks aren't doing anything rowdy or licentious—or illegal— are you?"

"Come on, man," Melville said curtly, shaking his head for

emphasis. "You know we do like to party a little. Nothing really heavy, though. No mushrooms or acid or stuff like that."

Phyllis suddenly shifted her attention to Peapod. "Last year. June. About a year ago now. You tried to slit your wrist. You wanted to commit suicide."

The young man rocked back on his bare heels, visibly startled by Phyllis's blunt frankness and what we others assumed must have been an accurate psychic impression.

"Yes, but I have been spiritually reborn since then," he said in a soft voice. "I feel that I'm on a good path now, studying the writings of Paramahansa Yogananda."

Phyllis nodded her approval. "That's good. Vibrations of suicidal thoughts would greatly disturb a gentle spirit such as the one that occupies this house. This spirit was one that truly loved life and who devoted her own life to working with people. She would be greatly offended by thoughts of someone taking his own life."

The psychic-sensitive now stood directly in front of the painting.

"Melville, you painted this after you smoked grass. It reflects your depression, your feelings of inadequacy, your fear that you are being tied down by your lack of formal training and education. You would like to be free and as individualistic as a unicorn. Yet you realized in your inner knowing that you will achieve artistic freedom only through discipline and training, not an unstructured existence that seeks to avoid commitment."

"Wow, heavy, man," Peapod agreed. "She nailed your butt, Mel. I told you that you should accept that scholarship and go back to college, man."

The psychic-sensitive nodded. "Do it, Melville. If you have such an opportunity to resume your formal training and education, you must do so."

"That would be so cool, babe." Shanti smiled. "I'll get a job as a waitress or something to help out."

At that moment of joyful recognition of a life's purpose, we were suddenly startled by a loud knocking on the wall next to the painting.

"Is there someone living in the room next door?" I asked, seeking first the rational explanation.

Melville was wide-eyed. "No, man. That's our storage room. Besides, everyone who's home now is downstairs watching the tube. They always show old movies at this time in the afternoon."

"*She* is pleased with your decision, Melville." Phyllis smiled. "The knocking on the wall was her signaling approval of your resuming your formal education. It has been her desire to turn you away from smoking grass and drinking alcohol and merely wasting your life. She has wanted to provoke you into a more serious application of your talent."

"But *who* is she?" Peapod insisted upon knowing.

"I think I might know," Matt interjected. "I did a little research on this place a few days ago when I knew for certain that Brad and Phyllis were coming."

Phyllis held up a hand to signal noninterference. "Please don't say anything just now, Matt. I'm picking up some strong impressions.

"I'm feeling that there was once a family who lived in this house that was very well connected in local society. They were, in other words, one of the important families in the city. I can hear them entertaining downstairs in the large room. I can hear a piano, violins, beautiful music."

"Oh, wow," Shanti had to interrupt. "I am getting goose bumps all over my body. I mean, how many times have we all heard music, especially piano music, in this house? And it always seems to be coming from that big room downstairs."

"Right on, babe," Melville agreed. "We've all heard it every once in a while."

Peapod nodded his silent agreement.

Phyllis seemed to be entering a light state of trance. "This was a very dignified high-class family," she went on. "And the daughter—the daughter . . . she's the one who plays the piano. A very elegant lady is she. And lonely. She's very lovely, but she is lonely. Ma-Ma-Mary . . . I almost had it. The *name*. I almost had it. *Marcella*!"

Phyllis's breath was coming in short gasps, as if she had been running up several flights of stairs. "Her parents die. She's an only child. She never marries. Her fiancé was killed in the war, World War One. She never loves another. She plays the piano. Teaches piano."

Matt could no longer contain himself. "She's right! She's bang on! The Rearden family built this house in 1896. He was a banker, a leading social light in the community. His daughter, Marcella, was a skilled pianist, almost went professional. She ended up being a piano teacher, and she lived here until she died in 1946. The house was next owned by a lawyer named Malanaphy, who sold it to the present owner, who let it sit empty for three or four years before these kids moved in."

"And her fiancé?" Shanti wondered. "Did he die in that terrible war? Was she lonely and alone?"

Matt shook his head. "I didn't find anything about Marcella Rearden's love life, but I do know that she was a spinster until her death."

Phyllis was speaking again, directly to Melville, Shanti, and Peapod. "The spirit of Marcella has manifested to provide you with spiritual balance. She is extending her influence to help you to learn better how to fit into the spiritual side of life so the material side will make better sense to you. She has seen the imbalances caused in some of you by the abuse of drugs and alcohol, and these violations of the spirit within you has greatly disturbed her. Feel her positive, loving energy moving all around you. Her gentle love will be able to help you achieve a wonderful transformation of body, mind, and spirit."

Shanti's mouth had formed a little red O of wonder. "It almost sounds like she wants to become our guardian angel."

"Or a spirit guide." Phillis smiled and nodded her agreement.

Late the next morning, just as I was preparing to leave my hotel to return home, I received an urgent call from Melville at the commune. "Please, man," he begged, "you've just got to come over here before you leave. It's nothing I can tell you about over the phone. You've just got to come see for yourself."

Phyllis had returned to her home the night before. Matt and I had seen her off at the airport after an enjoyable dinner at one of the city's better restaurants. Matt was swinging by the hotel to take me to the airport after he finished taping some public service announcements at the radio station.

"All right," I told Melville. "We'll squeeze some time out on the way to the airport."

On the drive to the commune Matt and I found it difficult not to speculate on what could have developed of such importance at the commune in the few hours since we had last been there.

Melville and Shanti were waiting for us on the steps to the grand old mansion.

"So what's up?" I got directly to the point, not wishing to miss my flight home.

Somewhat sheepishly, Melville explained that after we had left, he had addressed the unseen spirit of Marcella Rearden and asked for a sign that she really existed.

"I told him that that was a really boorish thing to do," Shanti said, rolling her eyes in embarrassment over her spouse's actions. "But what do *I* know?"

"Anyway," Melville said, thrusting an old, yellowed envelope into my hands, "this came in the morning's mail. We saw the postman put it in our mailbox just a few hours ago. That's when I called you, Brad."

It was a letter addressed in an elegant handwriting to Miss Marcella Rearden. The envelope bore a three-cent stamp and a postmark of July 13, 1928.

"And this was just delivered today?" Matt asked incredulously.

"In *today's* mail," Shanti repeated. "I mean, letters can get delayed and all, but the post office usually doesn't make mistakes like this. I mean, that's forty-two years!"

"And look," Melville added, just in case Matt and I had missed it, "that's forty-two years *to the day*!"

"What's the letter say?" Matt said.

"We haven't dared open it," Melville said. "That's why I called you, Brad. I mean, look, it's marked 'personal' and all."

I nodded, opened the letter. It was a notice from a department store in St. Louis, the one from which Marcella Rearden had apparently purchased her grand piano, reminding her that her piano was quite likely in need of tuning.

An eerie but not unpleasant sensation tickled my solar plexus. What a gentle yet provocative device by which to demonstrate one's continued survival after death—and one's continued interest in those who presently shared the house that she had loved so much in life.

I returned the letter to Melville and said, "I think it might be safe to assume that this most unusual manifestation from beyond is Marcella's way of telling you, my friend Melville, that you should waste no more time seeing to it that *your* instrument, your talent at painting, is 'tuned' and ready to go on with your life."

"And it probably wouldn't hurt to see that his spirit and his attitude get a good tuning while he's at it," his wife added.

"Such a tune-up is always a good thing," I agreed.

17. The Poor Boy Who Became a Millionaire by Following the Advice of His Spirit Teachers

During his early childhood on his father's eastern New York farm in the mid-1860s, Arthur Edward Stilwell was a sensitive boy who was given to daydreaming while he performed his daily chores.

By the time he was thirteen, he had acquired the ability to fall into altered states of consciousness and receive advice, admonitions, and prophecies from six spirits that had come to him as his ethereal teachers. Three of the entities told young Arthur that they had been engineers during their life experiences on Earth, two had been writers, and the sixth ghostly guide had been a poet.

On his fifteenth birthday Arthur was informed by his advisers in the spirit circle that he would be married in four years' time to a girl named Genevieve Wood.

"Nineteen is pretty young for a fella to be married," Arthur reminded his mysterious mentors. "Besides, I don't even know any girl by such a name. You folks are sure right about nearly everything that happens to me, but you are going to be 'way off target on this one."

After the spirits had finished giving him their nightly counsel and had faded back into the night shadows, the teenager got out of bed and wrote the name of his destined mate down in his diary.

"Genevieve, sweet Genevieve." He smiled as he dated the prediction. "The days may come and the days may go, but Genevieve is not going to show."

Four years later, just after his nineteenth birthday, Arthur found himself dancing with a pretty girl at a church festival.

"I've got to see you again," he told her as he brought her a cup of apple cider. "What's your name?"

"Jenny." She smiled. "Jenny Wood."

Arthur felt a tickling sensation in his solar plexus as he remembered the prophecy that his spirit teachers had made and the name that he had recorded in his diary.

"Jenny." He nodded over the rim of his cup. "I suppose that's a nickname for Genevieve?"

"No." She teased, shaking her head and crinkling her nose at him in a manner that completely delighted him. "It's a nickname for Hortense!"

Within a few weeks Genevieve Wood and Arthur Stilwell were married.

Even the most faithful believer of Horatio Alger rags-to-riches success stories or the most loyal fan of Frank Capra cinematic romanticism would not be easily persuaded to place his or her bet on Arthur Stilwell to make a millionaire of himself. He was out of school working as a printer's apprentice at fifteen, he had acquired a wife while still a teenager, and had recently gained employment as a commercial traveler with an insurance company.

But how many young men have the benefit of counsel from a circle of spirit teachers?

In the darkness they came to him. "Go west and build a railroad," they repeated night after night.

Young Stilwell protested. "I know nothing of railroads and high finance."

But still the ghostly voices beleaguered him. They kept at him so that he had to begin sleeping in a separate bedroom so he would not disturb his wife.

"Is—is it me?" Jenny wanted to know. "Have I done something to displease you?"

In the early days of their marriage Arthur did not dare discuss his invisible advisers with his bride for fear that she would think he was a couple of sandwiches short of a picnic.

"No, no, sweetheart," Arthur reassured Jenny. "Everything is fine between us, honest. It—it's the season that affects my allergies and clogs my sinuses. Every year at this time I really get stuffed up and I snore and sneeze like crazy all night long. I just don't want to disturb your sleep at night. It's only for a while."

As it turned out, the Stilwells slept in separate bedrooms for the rest of their long married life.

But as success followed success, Arthur was able to confide in Jenny and explain the necessity of his being able to confer with his guides in complete solitude throughout the night.

Yielding at last to the relentless demands of his spirit teachers, the Stilwells moved in 1887 to Kansas City, where he managed to find work with various brokerage firms.

With the nightly aid of his spirit teachers, Arthur was able to master the finer points of finance, and as amazing as it seemed to everyone—including himself—Stilwell was building his first railroad, the Kansas City Belt Line, before he was thirty-one.

Stilwell found that he had no difficulty in borrowing the money from the bankers, and upon completing the line a month ahead of schedule, he discovered that virtually overnight he had been transformed into a man who owned a rail-road worth millions.

Later, when Stilwell recorded this period of his life, he stated that such bold action required more nerve and self-confidence than he could have mustered by himself. He freely acknowledged that he could not have accomplished such fi-nancial feats without the advice and aid of his spirit teachers.

Often, when an engineering problem had him totally stumped, Stilwell would slip into a trance and awaken the next morning to find that the drawing board now bore the so-lution to his mental quagmire. The notes and drawings, ac-cording to Stilwell, were never in his own handwriting or drafting style.

Perhaps the most dramatic prophecy from his circle of spirit mentors occurred when they advised Arthur to build a railroad line from Kansas City to the Gulf of Mexico.

Stilwell was immediately impressed with the wisdom of such a move. A linkage of this sort would unite the midwest-ern farmers with the ocean steamships. Such a project not only would benefit the nation but could also prove very prof-itable.

Stilwell set out at once to turn the wheels of his highly ef-ficient organization into motion. Galveston, Texas, seemed to be the logical terminus of this new branch line, and he com-pletely immersed himself in the exciting new project.

However, for the first time in his life, he became so ab-sorbed in a new undertaking that he somehow managed to block out the regular visitations of his spirit teachers.

"I made the very human mistake of depending upon my-self and upon tangible things in my hour of need, forgetting the spiritual aid which was waiting and ready," Stilwell ad-mitted.

Then, as if the faithful spirits devised a last-resort method of forcing their fleshly protégé to slow down a bit and listen to them, Stilwell suddenly became ill.

With the boss in his sickbed, work on the railroad came to a halt, but Arthur was now in a position where he once again had to listen to his circle of spiritual advisers.

"You must *not* allow the new railroad line to go to Galveston," Stilwell was told.

Arthur frowned feebly from his sickbed. "But where else would I possibly locate the terminus?" he put the question bluntly to his ethereal tutors.

"That should be no problem for a man of your considerable wealth," he was told. "Build a new city. Name it Port Arthur."

Arthur snorted derisively and set himself to coughing. "Port Arthur, Texas," he said after he had taken several swallows of water. "People will not only say that I am vain—they will say that I am mad."

The spirit teachers were firm in their advice to steer the terminus away from Galveston: "Let them say what they will."

"Nothing your detractors can say will equal the disaster which will take place in Galveston if you allow your railroad to establish its terminus in that city."

"Not only will your life's work be ruined, but thousands of lives will be lost!"

Stilwell stirred uneasily in the bed where the "conference" was being held. He asked his spirit teachers exactly what they meant by uttering such ominous words.

"Look there on your bedroom wall," he was directed, "and you will see for yourself."

Stilwell watched in amazement as a misty picture of the city of Galveston began to form on the bedroom wall—swirling and wavering until it was at last focused with the clarity of a stereopticon slide. This most miraculous living photograph depicted people walking on the streets, going about their daily business.

The focus suddenly shifted to the docks of the seaport. Stevedores hustled up gangplanks with cargo; cranes dropped tons of wheat into open holds.

Then the brightness of the sky over the ocean became dark and troubled. From far out to sea a powerful hurricane began to work its way toward land, and as it made its way inexorably in the direction of Galveston, it churned the waters so that a powerful tidal wave arose from the depths of the ocean with the fury of a brutal, hulking beast of prey.

The monstrous wave gained momentum as it rolled faster and faster toward the shore and the seaport. It flung itself on the city of Galveston with the full fury of nature's power gone berserk. The Texas city was crushed, and large numbers of its populace were drowned.

When at last the horrible vision faded from the bedroom wall, Arthur Stilwell, damp with perspiration and totally convinced by the demonstration that his spirit teachers had presented, lay weakly back against the pillows.

"I shall build Port Arthur." He sighed, assuring the grim features of his ghostly advisors.

Stilwell returned from his sickbed completely rejuvenated. His first official action was to order the change in the course of his new railroad line. The boundaries of the city that would become Port Arthur were staked out in a vacant cow pasture. The precise location of the new municipality had been marked on a map by his spirit teachers.

True to Stilwell's own prediction, his critics shouted that he had gone insane when the new plans were announced.

The business associations and citizens' groups from Galveston violently protested the railroad baron's decision. They had been spared the terrible vision of the tidal wave that would crush the city. The only vision that concerned them was the one that showed them losing thousands of dollars in revenue to a city that had not yet been built.

Cautiously, in terms that he hoped they might be able to understand, Stilwell told them of his vision of the destructive hurricane and the great tidal wave.

As he had fearfully foreseen, his pronouncement angered Galveston's emissaries even more.

"It is bad enough that Stilwell has betrayed us," they grumbled, "but now he has the unmitigated gall to tell us that he changed his plans because of a bad dream!"

Then, of course, there were those who had hoped to turn a tidy profit from the sale of condemned lands along the site of the originally announced railroad route to Galveston. These speculators joined with Stilwell's enemies in Wall Street and brought the fight into Congress.

But Arthur Stilwell, with the constant encouragement of his spiritual advisers, held his ground and continued to finance both the completion of the new railroad line and the construction of Port Arthur.

In August 1900 an official ceremony christened Port Arthur the terminus for the Kansas City Southern Railroad. What had once been a useless swamp had been transformed into a canal that equaled the width and depth of the Suez. What had once been a cow pasture was now a proud new seaport where steamships could dock while awaiting trainloads of midwestern corn and wheat.

Only four days after the ceremonies which signaled the twin births of a railroad line and a seaport had been concluded, a powerfully destructive hurricane and tidal wave roared over the Gulf Coast, nearly demolishing the city of Galveston and killing more than six thousand of its citizens. The awful disaster had occurred just as it had been revealed years before to Arthur Stilwell by his spirit teachers. The massive tidal wave that smashed into Galveston was responsible for one of the greatest catastrophes in United States history, but by the time it reached Port Arthur across Sabine Lake, it was as mild as a ripple in a pond.

Once again the spirit circle had provided Stilwell with impressive proof of its existence and its unerring accuracy.

Because Stilwell had heeded the advice of his spirit teachers, Port Arthur was able to serve as a relief center for the stricken populace of its neighbor city. If he had followed his original plan and built his railroad terminal in Galveston, his empire would have been destroyed. Because he had listened to the counsel of his ethereal advisers, his personal fortune increased many times over.

Those who had once mocked him as a fool for erecting a city in the middle of a swampy cow pasture when an established seaport stood nearby eagerly awaiting the commerce of his railroad line were now hailing him as a genius, a visionary, and the luckiest man in the world.

Stilwell was always quick to point out that he had more than luck on his side.

As Arthur Stilwell became internationally known as one of North America's greatest empire builders, more and more people began to question him about his spirit teachers. Interestingly he was never one to theorize about his "friends." He felt no compulsion to attempt to explain how it was that he had the ability to interact with the spirit world. Stilwell never made a single effort to answer the whys and the hows of the skeptical.

In a very straightforward manner Stilwell stated that he was but an instrument for his spirit teachers, and they had been responsible for every financial investment and decision that he had ever made.

"My case is not all that unusual," he pointed out to those who seemed to meet his claims with incredulity. "Socrates, greatest of the Greek philosophers, used to give credit to his guardian spirit. Joan of Arc changed history by listening to her spirit teachers."

To those argumentative types who persisted in their skepticism, the multimillionaire simply stated that in his opinion the vast empire that he had built with the guidance of his spirit teachers offered the best kind of evidence of their existence.

Stilwell did, however, disclose to sincerely interested parties how he was able to contact the members of the spirit circle: "I lie down in bed alone in a dark room. I focus my mind on my immediate problem and allow myself to drift off into a sort of half sleep. I offer no resistance to any outside influence. Even though I am nearly unconscious, every plan, every diagram, chart, or map which is revealed to me during those moments is indelibly etched in my memory."

Stilwell went on to explain that his spirit tutors did not express themselves in a linear time sense. Past, present, and future were all one to them. They seemed to have access to all knowledge which issued from the Absolute, and they dictated their suggestions to him with utmost authority.

The vigorous millionaire was not an advocate of Spiritualism. In fact, shortly before his death Stilwell said that he had attended only one séance in his entire life and had been "bored to tears by it."

Neither did Stilwell have any association with any psychic research organizations or publicly endorse any of their theories. To the former country boy from Indiana, the relationship that he shared with his spirit teachers was a highly personal one, and other than offer sincere testimony of the essential role that they had played in his life, he never identified them beyond stating that the spirit circle was made up of three engineers, a poet, and two writers. His interaction with his companions from the world of the supernatural was as real and as vital to him as was his association with his earthly circle of friends, which included the likes of Henry Ford, George Westinghouse, and Charles Schwab.

Sir Arthur Conan Doyle, the creator of Sherlock Holmes and an indefatigable investigator of psychic phenomena, once said that Arthur Stilwell "had greater and more important psychic experiences than any man of his generation."

Arthur Stilwell lived to be sixty-nine and entertained himself in his twilight years by writing novels, articles, and motion-picture scenarios on an eight-hour-a-day schedule. According to the ambitious financier, this still left him plenty of time to manage his sprawling railroad empire and his numerous commercial interests.

Before Stilwell died on September 26, 1928, he had built the Kansas City Southern Railway; the Kansas City Northern Connecting Railroad; the Kansas City, Omaha, and Eastern; the Kansas City, Omaha, and Orient; the Pittsburgh and Gulf Railroad; and the Port Arthur Ship Canal. He had been responsible for the laying of more than twenty-five hundred miles of double-track railroad and, including Port Arthur, founded a total of forty towns.

His vast empire employed more than 250,000 persons and extended from the extensive railroad network to pecan farming, banking, land development, and mining.

In his spare time the millionaire wrote and published thirty books, nineteen of which were novels, among them the well-known *The Light That Never Failed*.

Arthur Edward Stilwell died clutching his wife's hand, confidently telling Jenny that he himself would soon be a member in good standing in the spirit circle.

18. Spirit Guides in Ancient Egypt—and in Modern Cairo

I shall never forget Cairo during evening rush hour.

As the afternoon darkened into twilight, it seemed as though badly battered automobiles from every junkyard in the world had been resurrected and given new life in the streets of the ancient Egyptian city. As my taxi driver wove our way through the impossibly heavy traffic, cars, bicycles, and pedestrians miraculously parted before him as if he were a latter-day Moses negotiating the Red Sea with the help of God. The streetcars and buses that we passed seemed so pressed with humanity that I could not imagine any of the passengers surviving the ride with all of their limbs, ribs, or vital organs intact.

Earlier that day, while visiting the mummy room in the Cairo Museum, I had met a most interesting man whom I'll call Mustafa, a local attorney who was interested in subjects of a metaphysical nature. We soon found ourselves in a lively discussion about spirit guides and teachers in the ancient world, and we had agreed to meet that evening for a cold bottle of Stella beer at an outdoor restaurant in the famous Khan El Kalili Bazaar and continue our conversation.

By the time that my stalwart cabdriver delivered me to the appointed restaurant, Mustafa had already arrived, and I was pleased to see that he had brought his wife, Lili, a Frenchwoman who many years before had come to Cairo to study and had fallen live with both the city and one of its citizens. A darkly attractive woman in her mid-thirties, Lili taught philosophy and French in a private school in the city.

After observing the basic amenities, I was eager to continue my research on the spirit guides of antiquity. I invited Lili to participate in the discussion if she wished. Then I received the couple's permission to tape-record our conversation.

Mustafa reminded me that from as early as the third millennium B.C. the written records of Egypt and Mesopotamia indicate that religious thought had already become complex in both belief and practice.

"Although as Europeans and Westerners we take great glory in the old Greek philosophers and like to credit them with the birth of intellectual thought," Lili pointed out, "it is really from the ancient Egyptians and Mesopotamians that we gain our first real insights into the human mind and its search for spiritual truths."

Mustafa nodded. "These ancient people recognized a hierarchy of supernatural beings that ruled over various parts of the Earth, the universe, and the lives of human beings. They also believed in lower levels of entities that might be either hostile or benign in their actions toward humans."

"Yes," I said. "There seems always to be a recognition, even among the most primitive of religious expressions, that there are the 'good guys' and the 'bad guys.' I suppose that is why the wise members of every priestcraft emphasize caution in attempting to invoke or summon these entities. It very often requires a great deal of wisdom and experience to be able to tell the difference between the positive and the negative."

Mustafa poured us each another glass of the dark Egyptian beer. "The ancient Mesopotamians wanted to be certain that they were well protected by their spiritual guardians. They called their guides, or genii, *shedu* and *lamassu.*"

Lili interjected a question for her husband. "Aren't the *lamassus* those rather grotesque creatures that look like lions or bulls with human heads and large wings? The ones that were often placed at the entrances of temples to ward off evil?"

"Like gargoyles on medieval churches?" I wondered.

Mustafa told us that we both were correct. "But not only were representations of these fearsome winged beings put in place to guard temples and palaces and so forth, but the common, ordinary people also considered them to be very accessible guardian spirits. There is, in fact, in a very ancient magical text of the Mesopotamians, an invocation that asks that the good *shedu* walk on one's right hand and the good *lamassu* walk on the left."

I said that I was familiar with the ancient Egyptian concept of the ka, the soul within us. "Did they also have an idea of a spiritual guardian or guide?"

Mustafa politely corrected me. "As I understand it, the ka was a kind of guardian angel. The ka, to the ancient Egyptians, was an invisible spirit double that was born with each individual and accompanied him or her on the pathway of life."

"Kind of like the Germanic concept of döppelgänger, the spiritual double?" Lili asked.

"Basically," Mustafa agreed. "But whereas the döppelgänger is simply a mirror image of oneself, the ka served more in the role of the guardian spirit or invisible protector."

I observed how interesting it was that all cultures had a tradition of a guardian spirit for each individual human soul.

"I have often pondered that fact," Mustafa said. "And I have wondered if there is something within us that requires an intercessor, an interpreter or messenger, between the Supreme Being and ourselves."

Lili had a theory to contribute. "In the earliest stages of religious thought there were usually a number of minor gods and goddesses to whom the people paid homage. There were nature spirits and water spirits and so forth in a great abundance. Maybe these ancient gods live on in our concept of guardian spirits. Maybe the nature spirits, the devas, have survived as our spiritual guides."

Mustafa considered his wife's speculation. "Perhaps as the great religious philosophies turned more and more toward monotheism, a one Supreme Being, the common folk required lesser entities to serve as their mediators between themselves and this one rather fearsome, almighty God."

Lili nodded, then added, "And we must not overlook the sad fact that things have always been tough down here on Earth. There have always been sickness and strife, death and taxes. It is very comforting to know that you have a guardian spirit who is looking out for you."

"Yes." I smiled. "Amidst all the trials and tribulations of Earth, it is comforting to know that someone up there likes us."

Mustafa chuckled. "Well, I know for a certainty that someone on the other side likes me. I know that I have a guardian spirit."

"Aha." Lili laughed. "Brad, you will now hear the story of Mustafa's torchbearer from the spirit world."

"By all means," I encouraged my newfound friend.

* * *

When he was just a boy of four or five, Mustafa was fasci-
nated by an elderly street peddler's cigarette lighter.

"He had bartered a phony artifact from an imaginary tomb
for an American soldier's Zippo lighter," Mustafa said, "and he
would brag that the lighter would never fail. He would even
accept bets from the street gamblers that it would be able to
light so many times in a row.

"Well, it got to be that gambling with the battered old
Zippo lighter became the old man's sole source of income,
and he became known in the streets as Torchbearer."

Mustafa's father had always preached that it was a blessing
to be kind to the poor, so the boy was always certain to perform some little act of kindness for old Torchbearer. Perhaps
he might bring him a bit of bread that he had not finished for
breakfast. Once, when he saw the old man's bare feet were
sore and bleeding, he donated a pair of his father's shoes to
the elderly peddler.

"I almost got a spanking for that act of kindness"—Mustafa
laughed—"for they were rather new shoes. But I reminded
my father that he had said that it was a blessing to treat the
poor with respect."

Old Torchbearer died when Mustafa was about nine. "I remember his friends telling me that they had buried him with
his beloved Zippo lighter. Everyone missed seeing Torchbearer around. He had always been a kind and cheerful man."

One night not long after the elderly peddler had passed
away, Mustafa made the mistake of taking an unfamiliar short-
cut home.

"I suddenly found myself in an alley that was so dark that
I could not see my hand in front of my face," Mustafa recalled.
"I was frightened out of my wits. What if I fell or was attacked

by stray dogs? What if I wandered all night, becoming more lost and confused by the minute?"

The boy was on the verge of tears when suddenly a flame flashed into a glowing ball of light beside him and drove back the darkness.

"It was Torchbearer giving me a light and guiding me to familiar territory," Mustafa said. "I could even smell the lighter fluid from his old Zippo."

Mustafa mentioned a number of other times when the guiding spirit of Torchbearer had manifested to give him reassurance and comfort.

The most dramatic occurred one stormy night when once again Mustafa, now nearly seventeen, was walking in a part of Cairo with which he was unfamiliar.

"This time the light manifested ahead of me, swaying back and forth like a railroad lantern. I had the distinct feeling that Torchbearer was signaling a warning to me."

Mustafa approached with great caution, and when he came to the place where the light had been hovering, he found some rotting boards covering an old, unused well.

"Before I realized fully what I was seeing, some of the rotten boards began to give way under my feet," Mustafa said. "Quickly I stepped back on solid ground. It seemed to take four or five seconds before I heard the sound of the pieces of wood hitting water below.

"There was no question that old Torchbearer had saved my life. It would have been unlikely that I could have survived such a fall, and it might have been days, weeks, or months before anyone would even have found my body in that ancient, unused well."

I asked Lili if she had ever seen Torchbearer's friendly flame.

She nodded, then smiled. "I used to laugh at such charming tales of ghosties and goblins, but I have seen the light of

Mustafa's spirit guide on two occasions. Once Torchbearer warned us not to enter a recent archaeological dig where a number of poisonous snakes had taken up temporary residence. I no longer doubt the fact that people really do have guardian spirits that look out for them."

19. Lalah, the Ghost That Struck Oil

Abram James was one of the most successful operators of oil wells in the early days of the petroleum business. Whenever he was asked to divulge the secret of his uncanny ability to locate oilfields, James unhesitatingly gave all the credit to Lalah.

And just *who* was this remarkable individual who was so incredibly proficient at locating previously untapped underground caverns of "black gold"?

Why, Abram James would tell you that, too. Lalah was a ghost.

James made his first oil strike in 1867 under conditions that the more conventional petroleum speculators would term strange.

He had been riding in a carriage with three friends midway between Titusville and Pithole City, Pennsylvania, when he suddenly leaped out of the vehicle and began to run across a farmer's field.

His friends halted the horses and set out on foot in pursuit of the swiftly running James, who they feared had surely gone mad. One moment he had been engaging them in quiet and polite conversation, and the next he was leaping over fences and gamboling about in a field.

When James reached the northern end of the field, he was seen by his companions to jerk convulsively, then fall to the ground. He was pale and rigid when they at last knelt beside him.

"Poor Abram has suffered some kind of fit, I fear," one of the men said, giving utterance to the mental confusion that they had all reached. "Look how pale he's become."

It was several minutes before James's eyelids began to flutter and he appeared to be resuming consciousness. "Dig here," he whispered.

"What is he saying? Why should we want to dig here in this farmer's field?"

"He's out of his head!"

"I knew he had been overworking."

James pushed aside the solicitous hands of his friends and sat up. "Lalah says to dig here."

"Who the devil is this Lalah?"

"*Devil* may be the correct identification. It's the spook that he claims is his guide."

"He's completely muddled. I warned him to stay away from Spiritualism and attending séances and such. For weeks now he's been saying that this lady spirit called Lalah has been whispering sweet nothings in his ear."

James stood up and faced his friends. "I know that you scoff at me behind my back for my beliefs, but Lalah has told me that there is oil here beneath the earth. You've all been friends of mine for many years. If you throw in with me and help me buy up this land, we'll all be rich men."

"Come along, Abram. You're not well."

James frowned his annoyance and shook off the arm that

one of his well-intentioned friends had draped around his shoulders. "I've never felt better, I'll have you know. And if you fellows know what's good for you, you'll take Lalah's advice and invest in my first oil well."

"We'll do no such thing. It seems blasphemous, almost obscene that you believe that some lady ghost carries on with you," another of his friends said indignantly.

James reached in a trouser pocket, pulled out a penny, and thrust it into the earth.

"Have it your way, then," he told his scoffing companions. "But this penny marks the spot where I will dig my first oil well."

His three friends continued to refuse the opportunity to invest in Lalah's oil well, and they tried their best to dissuade James from such nonsense.

Undaunted, Abram James borrowed money and bought the land from the farmer. So great was his faith in the advice of his spirit guide that he went even deeper into debt and obtained an additional loan to enable him to dig an oil well at the exact spot which he had marked with a penny.

His friends continued to jeer until the day when Harmonial Well No. 1 pumped up its first 130 barrels of crude oil.

According to the many astonishing stories told about Abram James, his unconventional technique for finding the "black gold" never varied.

Each time he was on land that covered oil deposits, he would be seized by Lalah and driven into a spasmodic dance which invariably ended with his falling to the ground on the exact spot where he later directed his crews to drill. As was his custom, James marked the spot with the same old worn penny.

In Abram James's long and prosperous career in the oil industry, the inspired instructions and the bizarre, tuneless choreography directed by Lalah, his spirit guide, are known to have produced only one dry well out of dozens of gushers.

20. The Nobel Prizewinner Who Received His Inspiration from the Spirit World

"Certain things had happened to me when alone in my room which convinced me that there are spiritual intelligences which can warn us and advise us," admitted William Butler Yeats, the winner of the Nobel Prize for literature in 1923.

Although Yeats has been often unfairly criticized for being "dream-headed and absentminded," the list of accomplishments which he achieved during his productive life shows the lack of truth in such criticism. He wrote thirty-five books of poetry, plays, essays, and criticism, organized the Irish Literary Society of London and Dublin, founded the Irish Literary Theatre, and served for seven years as a senator in the Irish Free State.

It was Yeats's desire to be a whole and a complete person that led him down the mysterious path of the mystic and brought him into contact with the most noted spiritualists and psychic-sensitives of his day. And while his passionate interest in the paranormal brought him a great deal of scorn from the more dogmatically traditional people of his day, he remained steadfast and unshaken in the face of criticism and rejection.

From his earliest childhood Yeats had a curiosity concerning the fascinating world of the occult. His mother told him fairy tales and folk tales while his father, J. B. Yeats, a pre-Raphaelite painter, provided him with an education befitting an artist.

Later, while he was still a very young man, Yeats's stimulated imagination led him to form the Dublin Hermetic Society with a group of friends, and not long thereafter he began a serious study of the occult with George Russell, who also wrote poetry under the pseudonym Æ. Within a very short time Russell's house had become a meeting place for young visionaries, artists, thinkers, and philosophers, all of whom shared Yeats's interest in the power of myth and symbol in human life.

Yeats had a favorite uncle who was a strong believer in the supernatural, and they would share visions whenever Yeats came to visit. On one occasion the uncle became ill with a fever, and Yeats was able to soothe him by simply thinking of the symbol of water.

The family doctor, who looked in on the uncle, was surprised to find him resting easily. When Yeats explained what he had done, the physician smiled and passed it off as simply a form of suggestion and hypnosis.

In his ceaseless quest for a new religion composed of equal parts of magic and myth, Yeats became a disciple of the famous Russian "mistress of the occult," Madame Blavatsky, and joined her Theosophist sect. He ignored all the many attacks launched against Blavatsky, and he never repudiated her philosophy—or its emphasis upon the value of intuition. Only when he was "excommunicated" from the Theosophists for a divergence of beliefs by Madame herself did Yeats finally quit the group.

In 1890, shortly after being asked to leave Madame Blavatsky's sect, he joined the Order of the Golden Dawn, which, among its members, included the notorious master magician Aleister Crowley. Yeats was really more at home with the Golden Dawn, because this occult group encouraged its members to practice active magic and to undertake experiments designed to demonstrate power over the material universe.

Becoming ever more a citizen of two worlds—the seen and the unseen—Yeats once made an invocation to the moon on seven nights in succession. He was finally rewarded with a vision of a centaur and a goddess shooting at a star with a bow and arrow.

People all over the area, some of them friends of Yeats, reported seeing the same manifestation at the same time. This particular remarkable incident later appeared many times in Yeats's poetry and in the verses of such friends as Arthur Symons.

Because of his earnest conviction that great truths could be acquired from the spiritual side of existence—truths which, in fact, could not be comprehended in any other matter—Yeats tirelessly investigated the ethereal domains of the magician, the alchemist, the seer, and the spiritualist medium. During each of his forays into the unknown, he hoped to understand more clearly the value and the power of symbolic images over humankind.

Yeats felt that spiritualist séances conducted by professional mediums were simply devices that might be employed by men and women of lesser psychic abilities who were incapable of inducing a vision by their own mental powers. However, at a séance which he attended before he had reached the age of twenty, Yeats had become so emotionally disturbed that he banged his head into the table and cried out as if he were in terrible anguish.

After this embarrassing incident he refused to attend another séance for many years and did not resume his visits to the spirit parlors until after he had met the astounding American medium Margery Crandon. The poet met the remarkable woman while on a lecture tour in the United States in 1910, and after sitting in her spirit circle for several sessions, he became reconvinced of the value of Spiritualism in one's quest to become a whole person.

Shortly after he married in 1917, Yeats and his wife began experimenting with automatic writing. To their collective surprise, Mrs. Yeats was extremely successful with this form of "spirit" communication, and the poet filled many of his notebooks with the inspired messages which were transmitted through his wife.

While on a lecture tour in California, Yeats made the propitious discovery that the spirit guide that regularly communicated through his wife via automatic writing was also capable of answering direct questions from him through Mrs. Yeats's voice while she lay sleeping. Such a direct pipeline to the spirit world proved to be a great asset to Yeats's exploration of the unseen dimensions, and his wife was also pleased by the new development, for the process of automatic writing was physically exhausting for her.

Yeats identified his personal guide as the spirit of Leo Africanus, who had been an actual person, a sixteenth-century traveler, poet, and geographer. The spirit entity's responses to Yeats's questions often came accompanied by strange sounds and peculiar, unexplainable odors.

Sometimes, according to the best of Yeats's attempts to describe the bizarre scents, they smelled something like snuffed candles. At other times the spirit manifestations were surrounded by the thick odor of flowers.

Although Yeats laid great stress on the value of communicating with the spiritualistic dimension of humankind, he came to trust no medium completely, with the exceptions of Mrs. Crandon and his own wife. The prizewinning poet sought truth above all else, and he soon came to recognize that hit-and-miss insights of many professional mediums.

Yeats's highly acclaimed verse could not help being affected by his arduous examination of the occult, and the imagery of his poetry is strongly influenced by the remarkable experiences that he shared with the uncharted world of the paranormal.

"The mystical life is the center of all that I do and all that I think and all that I write," he once freely confessed.

And it was that very supernatural center of *all* that he did that helped him to produce the body of work that was judged worthy of the Nobel Prize in literature in 1923.

21. Clark Gable's Mysterious Otherworldly Encounter

A truly remarkable cast had been assembled for *The Misfits*, which boasted an original script that the Pulitzer prizewinning playwright Arthur Miller had written for his wife, Marilyn Monroe. In addition to Ms. Monroe, the players included Montgomery Clift, Eli Wallach, Thelma Ritter, Estelle Winwood, Kevin McCarthy, and Clark Gable, the ruggedly handsome leading man who years before had been internationally acclaimed as the "King" of Hollywood motion pictures.

Unfortunately, in spite of excellent performances by the actors, who had been directed by the highly acclaimed John Huston, the film was not a great success. The poor reception of *The Misfits* by both the critics and the moviegoing public is made even more poignant by the fact that the film features the last cinematic appearances for both Monroe and Gable.

Clark Gable, the King, the charismatic actor who had created so many memorable screen performances, died at the age of fifty-eight in November 1960—before the picture's release and the birth of his first and only son.

Gable did not begin his long film career as a Hollywood monarch. Like so many other actors, he had to pay his dues by knocking on doors, working at any job that would keep him alive until he could do what he really wanted to do, and appearing in a seemingly endless number of bit parts until someone noticed his screen presence.

Although Gable never underplayed his years of struggle, he also acknowledged the importance that a mysterious mystical encounter had made in turning both his life and his career around and setting him upon a more positive path.

Clark Gable's first real opportunity in acting came in 1928, when he was about twenty-seven years old and was given the leading role in a drama entitled *Machinal* that was to play on Broadway.

The young actor was eager to show his talent and ability, and for weeks he exhausted himself at the mentally and physically enervating rehearsals. He held nothing back, and soon the emotional ravages of the play began to exact harsh payment from his personal life.

Finally, his body weakened by constant fatigue, his mind foggy from the constant outpouring of his emotions, he began to doubt the reality of his hopes of becoming an actor.

On a cool Friday evening Clark Gable decided to go for a long walk to review his prospects in life. After hours of treading the sidewalks in a kind of altered state of consciousness, he realized that he had wandered out on a pier down on the waterfront.

He had not been there long, gazing out at the boats in the harbor, when a down-on-his-luck vagrant approached him.

"What are you doing here?" the bum asked him.

Gable shrugged. "Going for a swim, I guess."

The tramp scrutinized the actor carefully, then spoke again: "You won't be needing those clothes where you're going. Take 'em off."

Gable recalled that he offered the vagrant no argument and slowly stepped out of his clothing. It was evident that the street person was in desperate need of new garments, so without a word the two men exchanged apparel.

"How about your money?" the tramp asked.

Gable chuckled. "All I've got is thirty bucks, pal. You're welcome to it. Now leave me alone, please. Good-bye."

The two men parted, and Gable continued his walk down the pier in the bum's ragged clothing.

The young actor had not gone much farther when he met another man. This fellow was older than the tramp, with a gentle look in his eyes. And even though his clothes were a bit on the shabby side, it was apparent that his suit had once been a fine one and even now seemed fresh and clean.

Most of all, though, Gable was struck by a certain "ineffable something" that seemed to exude from the stranger. It was as if the man had come from another world.

"Young man," the stranger confronted him, "where, may I ask, are you going?"

"I'm going for a swim," Gable answered once more.

"Not a good idea." The man shook his head. "Why don't you come home with me instead?"

The suggestion seemed a reasonable one to the actor's somewhat befuddled mind, and he saw no point in refusing the unexpected invitation.

Gable followed the man on a most confusing route to his home. The journey was so bewildering that he had no idea where they were once they finally arrived at their destination. In spite of all that, Gable felt immediately comfortable in the simple, homey atmosphere of the place. He relaxed and allowed the tranquillity that radiated from the man's home to permeate his entire body.

Gable was completely unprepared for the sudden appearance of his host's daughter, however. The young woman astounded the future Hollywood male sex symbol with her beauty and quiet grace. The young actor was received warmly by her, without a trace of pretense.

Later, after a delicious meal, she placed a gentle kiss on Gable's forehead before she retired for the evening. He was impressed with the guilelessness of the act.

After his daughter had gone to bed, Gable found that his host was ready to do some serious talking.

"Many years ago," he began, "I was a very famous and wealthy man. I was fortunate enough to be married to a woman I loved above all others. But, my young friend, I learned that material possessions are only on loan to us for a very short duration. Eventually we must return them all.

"So it was that I gave away first my fame, then my money. Finally, I gave personalized love away."

The kindly gentleman's voice was smooth and unbroken as he spoke of the sacrifices that he had made in his life and the humility that he had learned.

He warned the actor about the fickleness of the public and how quickly its fancies passed from one person to another.

He spoke of the dangers of too much money and the lure of indiscriminate sex.

"You must always cling to the higher values in life," he cautioned Gable, "for they are the only enduring things in this quixotic world."

His host spoke on, quietly, resonantly.

Slowly it began to dawn on Gable that the man was describing his own future years, allowing them to unfold before him one by one. As he sat in a strange place that he did not recognize, listening to a man he had never seen before, Gable realized that he was being presented with a blueprint to follow if he was to achieve his life's goals.

Clark Gable lost all sense of time and place as he listened spellbound to the older man's wisdom and advice. After so long, though, his sensory impressions began to swirl around inside his head, and he could no longer determine what was real and what was illusory.

When the actor regained normal consciousness, he was lying on his bed back in his apartment. He was amazed to learn that it was Monday morning.

Somehow he had completely lost three days of his life.

Although his head was still spinning from his weird experience, Gable got out of bed, cleaned up, and headed for rehearsal.

Later, during his noon lunch break, Gable was walking toward his regular restaurant when suddenly, through the throng of people, he saw his elderly host's daughter.

A surge of emotion welled up within him as he hurried toward her and called out her name.

The young woman did not respond but continued on her way.

At last Gable caught up with her and reached for her arm. He was completely startled when his hand went through thin air.

The girl was no longer there.

She had vanished.

Clark Gable first told this story many years ago to Dana Howard and Art Solomon of Ullman Publications. As he concluded this bizarre tale, he could not help musing: "There in that place where there was neither money nor the urgent need to struggle for material things, I felt a sense of peace and

happiness approaching the supernatural. That strange inter-
lude influenced me beyond anything that I have ever experienced.

"In those three days that I lost out of life, I found myself."

22. With an Angel of Light as Her Ally, She Fought a Duel with a Demon

The Malagasy called her Ninebe, "The Great Mother."

It was an appellation which I knew that Ingara Nakling had earned in her more than three decades of missionary work in Madagascar. Whether she was looking after the parentless in the mission orphanage, leading a hymn sing in a jungle clearing, or administering a bromide from her first-aid kit, Ingara had set an example for her adopted people.

When I first met Ingara, she was already eighty-five years old. I found this hard to believe because she was still robust and filled with cheerful energy. As I visited with her, I marveled at the facility with which her mind could relate anecdotes about events which had taken place during the first days of her arrival in Madagascar when she was but a young woman in her early thirties.

"There is no word in the Malagasy language for 'love,'" she said, indicating but one of the many challenges that confronted her in communicating with the native people. "Love is central to the Christian faith. It would be impossible to tell of Jesus without telling of his great love for all humankind. It was therefore necessary to combine existing word concepts. The Malagasy had words for 'fear' and 'hate' because their old gods were deities of hate, not love."

When missionaries arrive in a strange land, they find that they are instantly on the spiritual firing line. Missionaries have been slaughtered and all Christians persecuted in areas where an overzealous cleric offended the indigenous culture by a rash or clumsy act. Shortly before Ingara arrived in Madagascar, a Roman Catholic priest was slain when he made the mistake of ripping a charm from the neck of a tribal chieftain.

"You have to learn to know the people," Ingara told me. "You must learn their thinking. Most of all, you must show love."

Although she had won the hearts of many of the native tribespeople and had come to be known as the Lady Who Loves People, in addition to being called the Great Mother, she confided that she had not always been confident during her experiences in the field. There was the time, for instance, when she was confronted with her first case of demon possession.

It was quite late at night when she was aroused from her meditations by an urgent knocking on her door. There she found several of her carriers, one of whom was a Christian convert and a member of her congregation. He was the man whom she trusted to provide her with transportation through the jungle.

"Please come with us, Ninebe," begged the man.

Ingara followed the men outside and was soon confronted by the bizarre spectacle of one of the native bearers crawling toward her porch on his hands and knees.

"He has been possessed by a demon," the man nearest her whispered hoarsely.

"Cast the demon out of me, Ninebe," whined the afflicted

one, who had by now reached her knees. "Cast him out, and I'll lick your feet!"

"That won't be necessary," the missionary told the man, involuntarily moving her feet several inches away from his slavering jaws.

Ingara Nakling, Lutheran missionary lady, was confused. She had heard all the learned dissertations about "demon possession" being but a primitive expression for mental illness. She had no doubt that this might often be the case.

Yet she sincerely believed that possession could be a very real thing apart from a mental aberration. And she sincerely believed that an essential element in the mission of Jesus on Earth was to cast out demons. After all, did he not give his followers his own promise that they could also cast out demons in his name?

And in the infinite duality of life on Earth, she knew there were angels of light and good. Did not that truth suggest that there were also angels of darkness and evil?

"My stomach!" wailed the man as he bent double with pain and collapsed on the ground at her feet. "The demon is in my stomach!"

Ingara Nakling hesitated. She was still undecided. "I'll get you a bromide." .

"That will do me no good! Cast out the demon," the man pleaded.

Her converted carrier stepped close to her and explained to her in hushed whispers that the man had been sent to her as a challenge. The witch doctor in the demon-possessed victim's village had enlisted the aid of strong men to hold him down and pry open his mouth so that he might pour "devil medicine" down his throat.

"The witch doctor fears that you are becoming too powerful," the convert told her. "He fears your power of love, and he does not want to lose his control over the people.

"Everyone knows that he has sent a demon into this man. If you cannot cast out the evil spirit, all of the villages will see that the witch doctor and the old gods are more powerful than you and your God of love."

Ingara looked closely at the man's face. There was *something* about his eyes—something very different from the glaze caused by either mental imbalance or a gastrointestinal disturbance.

She made her decision. She sent one of the men for the native evangelist and ordered the other men to carry the moaning carrier into the house.

Then, while a number of older village girls who stayed with her sang hymns, the missionary lady began to prepare for the ordeal, the duel with the witch doctor's demon.

It was a violent session of intense prayers with both Ingara Nakling and the native Evangelist beseeching the God of Love to cast out the demon that tormented the contorted man who lay before them.

During the course of the exorcism the demoniac's body levitated several inches into the air. The missionary lady kept her hand on the man's head and only increased the fervor of her prayers when his trembling body floated free of the bed.

At last the man was quiet, and after a time his eyes flickered open and he appeared to have regained consciousness.

"Do you know me?" she asked him.

The man grinned. "You're the Lady Who Loves People! And you have chased the demon out of my stomach."

Ingara uttered a brief prayer of thanksgiving. The ordeal was over. The witch doctor's challenge had been met. And she, with the help of the native Evangelist and God, had won.

"From that day on, the native witch doctors used to look at me with bullhead eyes," Ingara remembered with a chuckle. "I grew bolder in dealing with those poor victims whom the witch doctors had possessed with their angels of darkness."

Ingara Nakling's stalwart spirit led her into many more duels with tribal priests who sought to summon demons to do their negative bidding of control over the people of the villages.

It was a day of triumph for the forces of light when one of her most powerful foes among the witch doctors presented himself at her doorstep and declared that he wished to cease his traffic with the creatures of darkness and to join her in serving the God of Love and the angels of light.

Ingara Nakling lived out the remainder of her days in South Dakota in a house that was filled with the echoes and memories of Madagascar and the people who came to return her love and respectfully name her their Great Mother.

23. His Murdered Son's Voice Led Him to the Killer

In 1970 twenty-six-year-old Bobby Reider of Melrose Park, Illinois, was murdered on his mother's birthday, April 26.

The victim's uncle, John Reider, had the sad task of notifying Bobby's parents, Mark and Joan Reider, and his seventeen-year-old sister, Marge, who lived in a suburb of Philadelphia.

Mark answered the telephone, and the moment that he heard his brother's voice, he knew the news was going to be bad.

"Mark, get a grip on yourself now," John told him. "There is no easy way to say this. Bobby has just been found murdered."

John told him that the police had no leads at the present time. Bobby had been found in a vacant lot near a condemned warehouse in a run-down area near Chicago. He had been shot three times in the stomach.

Mark felt his head spinning as the terrible news struck him with its full impact.

He told his brother that he would call him later. Then he put down the receiver and was left with the awful task of informing his wife and daughter that the life of their beloved son and brother had been snuffed out by a person or persons unknown.

Somehow, even above the sound of their cries and tears and the blinding sting of his own sorrow, Mark knew that his son's death had something to do with the Corvette automobile that Bobby had just sold to someone who had given him a bad check for the amount.

Only a few days before, Bobby had called home to ask his advice about how to handle the matter. Mark had advised him to give the fellow a second chance to made his check good, but if he still didn't get his money, then he should call the police.

Bobby, Mark vowed silently, *I'll find whoever did this to you. He won't get away with it. I promise that I'll find him and bring him to justice.*

In less than an hour Mark, Joan, and Marge were packed and on their way to John's home in Melrose Park, Illinois, to arrange for Bobby's funeral.

For ten silent, grim hours the Reider family sat quietly in the car, each alone with his or her respective memories of the young man who had been a good student and had also excelled in athletics—first in Little League, then in football and baseball in high school. Just last year Bobby had received an honorable discharge from the Army after completing a tour of duty in Germany.

When Mark and John Reider went to the morgue to claim Bobby's body, the authorities tried to be as kind as possible. Although Bobby had been dead for about six hours before a policeman on patrol had discovered his body, the autopsy showed conclusively that Bobby had died instantly after being shot in his stomach.

As Mark stood there looking down at his son, a strange thing occurred to him. Although his family had always been a religious one with extremely orthodox beliefs, Mark suddenly heard Bobby's voice speaking to him.

"I've never believed in ESP or anything of that sort," Mark said pointedly. "And I've always thought that spiritualist mediums were probably communicating with demons, but I swear that I heard Bobby say, *'Oh, Dad, thank you so much for coming here to this terrible place. I know everything will be all right now.'* "

A few hours later after seeing to the funeral arrangements, Mark paid a visit to Detectives Jerry Hamel and Mike Nintzel, the two officers who were in charge of the homicide investigation. The men were sympathetic to Mark's loss, but they had to admit that they really had no clues to his son's murder.

"We were hoping that maybe you could provide us some clue—anything at all—that might give us something to go on," Hamel said.

"You don't have a thing?"

Nintzel shook his head no. "As you know, that area is pretty run-down and deserted. Just old warehouses, empty lots, and piles of trash. A couple of transients who had been drinking wine in one of the deserted buildings said that the only thing they had seen all day was someone driving around in a red sports car sometime before they passed out."

"My son's car!" Mark told the detectives. "That must have been Bobby's red Corvette that he was talking about. Someone had given him a bad check for the car. He called me just a few days ago, wondering what he could do about it."

Detective Hamel wrote down the description of the Corvette incident to the best of Mark's recollection of his telephone conversation with Bobby. "Thank you, Mr. Reider," he said. "You just may have given us our first lead."

Mark Reider left the police station intending to drive back to his brother's house and pick up Joan. They had decided that they wanted to visit a shopping mall and purchase suitable clothing for Bobby's burial. They had already visited his apartment and found primarily informal clothing—jeans, sport shirts, a couple of jackets. They wanted him to be buried in a new suit.

As he drove through the city, Mark suddenly felt an eerie premonition that an automobile very important to Bobby and his murder would very soon come over the crest of the hill on the left lane. Simultaneously with this intuitive knowing came the voice of his murdered son, as clearly as he had ever heard it in life: *"Get ready, Dad. Be alert. There he is. He's coming over the crest of the hill. The one who murdered me!"*

Mark's heart began to pound his chest with quickening thuds when he saw a red Chevrolet Corvette coming his way. He got a quick glimpse of a young man at the wheel before he swung his own car into a U-turn and headed after the Corvette.

Mark was very cautious for the next half mile or so. He was careful to stay about five hundred feet behind the sports car so the driver did not suspect that he was being followed.

"Good going, Dad," Bobby told him. *"You're doing great. Just hang back. He knows his way around these streets. If he suspects he's being followed, he could shoot down a side street and lose you."*

The driver of the Corvette appeared to be oblivious of the startling fact that the father of his victim was in close pursuit.

"Watch it, Dad. He's going to pull over up ahead there. Just take it easy and stay calm."

Just as Bobby predicted, the red Corvette pulled up behind a parked car in front of a fast-food restaurant. *"The creep works here. Watch him, Dad!"*

Mark swung into the parking place just in front of the Corvette, so that the driver would be effectively blocked both front and back.

"Watch him, Dad, he's armed. He's still got the gun,"

Bobby said as Mark got out of his car and approached the other driver.

Mark was somewhat surprised to see how young the man was, barely out of his teens. He was not much over five feet seven or eight, and he had a very slender frame.

"Excuse me." Mark hailed him, trying to keep his voice from trembling with rage. "Isn't that Bobby Reider's car that you're driving?"

The young man turned, studied Mark coldly before he answered, "Yeah, it *was* his car. So? What's it to you, mister?"

The young man seemed totally unperturbed, completely in control of his emotions.

"I'm his father—Bobby's father."

A slight smile tugged at the man's thin lips. "Oh, yeah, Bobby's old man from back East someplace. Pennsylvania, right? I saw the car with the Penn plates in front of Bobby's uncle's place. I guess you're here for the funeral, huh? I read in the papers about the terrible thing that happened to Bobby. Too bad. He was a good guy."

Mark found it unfathomable that anyone could be so cool and unemotional after having killed a man a few days before. A major part of him wanted to throw himself on the little weasel and beat him senseless—maybe even to death.

"Steady, Dad. Just take it easy."

"Well, I'm Dave Murphy. I bought Bobby's car a couple of weeks ago. He must have told you."

"Watch him, Dad. Be careful! Help is on the way. Just be cool!"

"Bobby told me that you gave him a bad check."

Murphy shrugged. "I made good on it."

"Do you have the title to prove it?" Mark pressured him.

"Sure, I got the title." Murphy sneered. "You want I should show it to you?"

"I would certainly appreciate it," Mark told him.

"Watch it, Dad! He's got a gun in the glove compartment!"

With Bobby's warning sounding in his ears, Mark told Murphy to forget the title. "I'm just curious. How did you make the check good? Another check?"

"Naw, I paid him cash. I figure that must have been what got him killed," Murphy said. "He must have had the money on him, and he got robbed and shot."

Mark's hands began to open and close spasmodically. They were strong hands, hands that had been toughened by years of hard physical labor. It would be so easy once he got his hands around Murphy's scrawny neck!

At that moment Detective Hamel and a uniformed officer braked a police car to a stop just in back of the two men.

As the officers approached them, Mark pointed to Dave Murphy and shouted: "This is the man who killed my son! That's Bobby's car. Search it, and you'll find a gun in the glove compartment."

Dave Murphy's practiced veneer of cool began to shatter when the uniformed police officer pulled a .38 automatic from the glove compartment of the Corvette. Amazingly, three spent shells still lay on the floor of the car. The cocky young punk hadn't bothered to dispose of the evidence. He had probably even been bragging about the murder to his friends.

"There are some drops of blood on the armrest on the passenger side," Detective Hamel said. "I'll take any odds that we'll find the blood to be Bobby's type."

Later, after Dave Murphy had confessed to the murder of his son, Mark learned that Murphy had picked Bobby up after work with the promise that he would give him cash for the bad check. Instead he had driven him to the area of condemned and abandoned warehouses and murdered him.

Mark Reider was given credit for bravely detaining his son's murderer until the police arrived to place him in custody. Mark, however, knew that the credit belonged to Bobby's spirit that had somehow managed to communicate with him as if he were physically there beside him.

"How *was* it that you happened to drive up at the moment when Murphy was probably getting ready to reach for his gun and kill me?" Mark Reider asked Detective Hamel after Bobby's funeral.

Hamel smiled and shook his head slowly. "That was a funny thing. Actually I had slipped back to the locker room in hopes of catching a little nap. I was just dozing off when I got the strongest impression that you somehow needed my help. I knew I couldn't explain that to anyone, so I just corralled this rookie cop and told him to drive me along the route that I figured you would be taking to your brother's place. And there you were in a standoff with your son's murderer."

Mark Reider told his family about Bobby's communication from beyond, but he said that he has made no further effort to contact his son's spirit.

"Neither has he ever spoken to me again," he said. "I guess that means that our Bobby is now resting in peace."

24. A Dead Sea Captain Kept the Ship from Destruction

"At some future day it will be proven—I cannot say when and where—that the human soul is, while in earth-life, already in uninterrupted communication with the living in another world; that the human soul can act upon these beings and receive, in return, impressions of them without being conscious of it in the ordinary personality," stated the great philosopher Immanuel Kant.

In *Death and Its Mystery* (1923), Camille Flammarion recounted a story of two souls—one of the living, the other of the dead—that had somehow maintained a spiritual contact with each other that resulted in a communication that saved a ship and its crew from almost certain death and destruction.

Quoting directly from the statement of Captain Drisko, who was the principal witness to the incident, Flammarion repeated the essential passages that dealt with the near shipwreck of the *Harry Booth* that occurred while on a voyage between New York and the Dry Tortugas in 1865.

* * *

After he had completed an inspection of the bridge and sat-isfied himself that everything was as it should be, Captain Drisko turned the command over to his first mate, "an abso-lutely trustworthy officer," and retired to his cabin for a little rest.

At ten minutes to eleven Captain Drisko heard very dis-tinctly a voice shouting at him to return to the bridge and give orders to cast anchor.

Demanding to know who was bold enough to be issuing such orders to the captain of the ship, Captain Drisko ran back up on the bridge to find the cheeky culprit.

Once up above, Captain Drisko was surprised to find every-thing as it should be. And nobody admitted to having seen anyone go down to his cabin.

Supposing that he had been "the dupe of an auditory illu-sion," Captain Drisko went back down to his cabin to rest.

At ten minutes to twelve he was startled when a man dressed in a broad-brimmed hat and a long gray overcoat walked unannounced into his cabin.

"Gazing at me fixedly, he ordered me to go up and have the anchor cast," Captain Drisko stated in his written account of the incident. "Thereupon he went away calmly, and I heard distinctly his heavy steps as he passed in front of me."

Increasingly baffled by the actions of the bold intruder, Captain Drisko went back up to the bridge, but once again he was unable to perceive anything out of the ordinary.

"Everything was all right—and since I was absolutely sure of my course, I had no reason for heeding a warning, no mat-ter from what quarter," he wrote.

Captain Drisko went back to his cabin, but no longer with the intention of catching a brief nap. He remained dressed and at the ready, just in case there might really be need of his command. The recent run of bizarre activities had his nerves on edge and had placed him on alert.

At ten minutes to one Captain Drisko was astonished to see the same man in the broad-brimmed hat once again enter his cabin and order him, "in authoritative tones," to go up on the bridge and give orders to cast the anchor.

It was then that Captain Drisko recognized the intruder. "It was my old friend Captain John Burton, with whom I had gone on voyages as a boy—and who had been extremely kind to me."

Understanding at last that a dire necessity had summoned his mentor from the grave to warn him to cast anchor, Captain Drisko stated: "With one bound I reached the bridge and ordered the sails lowered and the anchor cast.

"The sea, where we were, was fifty fathoms deep. It was in this way that the vessel *Harry Booth* escaped running on the rocks of Bahama."

With heartfelt gratitude, Captain Drisko gave thanks to the memory of Captain John Burton, a long-dead protector, whose ceaseless and urgent demands to cast anchor had saved his onetime apprentice's ship from being wrecked on the deadly rocks off the Bahamas.

25. Adrift for Six Months, the Two Fishermen Were Saved from Death by the Ghost of Their Friend

In the summer of 1991 three fishermen—Tabwai Mikaie, Nweiti Tekamangu, and Arenta Tebeitabu—set out on a fishing trip from their South Pacific island of Kiribati, in the Republic of Kiribate.

Not far from land, off a coral atoll called Nikunau, they were suddenly pummeled by a powerful, unexpected cyclone that capsized their twelve-foot boat and tossed them into the sea.

Although the men lost their outboard motor, they managed to climb safely back into the boat. However, since they were no longer able to power the tiny vessel, they began to drift farther and farther out into deeper waters, thus commencing a voyage that at times must have seemed endless.

Incredibly the three men remained adrift for 175 days and nearly a thousand miles.

By using a spear and a fishing line, they were able to survive on fish. From time to time they achieved some variety in their diet when they were able to snare a coconut floating by.

To supplement their meager water supply, they collected rain-water.

On numerous occasions razor-jawed sharks circled their boat, sizing them up for dinner, but the fishermen turned the tables on the monsters and caught and ate no fewer than ten of the voracious predators during their six months adrift.

Tabwai Mikaie, twenty-four, said that they prayed to God four times a day, asking for his tender mercies to save them.

Tragically, after a seeming eternity of helpless drifting, Nweiti Tekamangu, forty-seven, died when they were at last in sight of land.

Although his friends wept and pleaded with him to hold on for just a few days longer, Tekamangu's heart simply gave out after such a strenuous ordeal, and his sorrowful companions had no choice other than to cast his body overboard.

The survivors, Tabwai Mikaie and Arenta Tebeitabu, were now terrified by the thought of the formidable ordeal that lay before them. Since they were now only a few days from the mountainous island of Upolu in Western Samoa, they would soon have to maneuver their little twelve-foot boat through some of the most treacherous reefs in the South Pacific. In their weakened condition, the task seemed impossible.

Tekamangu, the oldest of their tiny crew, had also been the most experienced and by far the most accomplished naviga-tor. If he were still alive, they cried out to each other in their anguish, he would have had the necessary skills to guide them to a safe harbor.

Mikaie and Tebeitabu began to resign themselves to what appeared to be their certain destiny: They, too, would perish before they reached land.

Just as it seemed certain that their boat would be shattered into a thousand pieces of driftwood, the two men were aston-ished to see the spirit of their dead friend rise from the depths of the turbulent sea.

"Just listen to me, and you will be safe," the ghost of Tekamangu told them authoritatively.

Although there were sharp and treacherous reefs on each side of their weather-beaten and sea-battered boat, Mikaie and Tebeitabu placed their complete confidence in the commands of their ghostly comrade, who masterfully guided them through the murderous offshore rocks to the safety of the beach on Upolu.

Soon the two skeletal, half-dead fishermen were being lifted from their little boat and taken to a hospital.

Later, while authorities and journalists decreed the feat of their having survived six months adrift at sea as a miracle, Tebeitabu and Mikaie testified that only the supernatural presence of their friend had allowed them to live.

In their fervent statements to the authorities they declared that if Tekamangu's love and loyalty had not sent his spirit back to help them, they would surely have been dashed to splinters on the reefs of Upolu. After six months adrift at sea, they, too, would have perished just a few miles from land.

26. Who Piloted the B-24 Back to Its Base?

War powerfully alters the psychological atmosphere of those nations in conflict, and perhaps for the first time for many individuals, the fear of violent death turns the thoughts of great masses of men and women toward the spiritual aspect of existence.

I have been told many remarkable accounts of guiding spirits saving the lives of servicemen and -women during their confrontations with the Grim Reaper on the battle lines of numerous wars. Few can equal the following account of a ghost that flew a bomber home.

Captain Brick Barton of Auburn, New York, was the pilot of a B-24 bomber out of an English base in World War II. On the day in question Barton and his crew had just completed their bombing mission over Frankfurt, Germany.

"All targets approached and all eggs dropped from the basket, sir," said the copilot. "Now we can go home."

Captain Barton agreed. "And we've done a darn good job,

too. It sure will be good to set down on the old terra firma again. This has been a tough mission, and I am bushed."

As Captain Barton was in the process of heading the bomber back toward England, a German fighter seemed to come from nowhere and made a strafing pass at the B-24. The pilot's compartment was riddled, and several bullets struck Barton.

The copilot, seeing that his captain had been hit, took immediate control of the plane. "Sir, are you all right?"

The copilot could hear the harsh chatter of the B-24's machine gunners, and he knew that he would not have to worry about the German fighter any longer.

But if Captain Barton were seriously wounded, he anxiously asked himself, just how would *he* be able to get the giant bomber all the way back to England all by himself?

He was a greenhorn, a replacement for Barton's former copilot, who had caught a million-dollar wound on a previous run and been sent back stateside. He was the first to admit that he was still wet behind the ears.

The young copilot knew that his training had been rushed because of the intense war effort and that he was really too inexperienced to have been assigned to fly beside a veteran pilot like Brick Barton. And he had never flown solo on a mission over Hitler's backyard and back to Britain.

"Don't worry, kid," Barton told him. "I'm all right."

"But you're hit, sir!"

"Hey, come on." The captain grinned at him. "It only hurts when I laugh. Sure, I caught a couple of slugs from that Jerry's guns, but they didn't affect my jaw any. Maybe I can't use my arms so well, but I can still talk."

Captain Barton leaned back in his seat. "I'll tell you what, kid. You just stay on the controls, and I'll give you first-class instructions all the way back to the base. How does that sound?"

The young copilot was greatly relieved. "I know I can do it if you tell me how."

"You got the spirit, kid," the captain assured him. "You'll get us home all right. I'll be with you all the way."

Later, as the B-24 neared the British base, the copilot radioed the tower and told it to prepare an ambulance for Captain Barton. Continuing to follow his skipper's detailed instructions, the copilot accomplished a perfect landing.

When the relieved young officer stepped out of the bomber, the waiting flight surgeon complimented him on a safe landing.

"Thank you, sir," he said, "but I couldn't have done it without the help of Captain Barton. He kept talking to me and giving me pointers from the moment he was hit in Frankfurt to the second we touched down on the landing field. You had better see to him right away. I'm afraid his wounds are more serious than he lets on."

The flight surgeon nodded and hurried into the pilot's compartment to check on Captain Barton at once.

A few minutes later, visibly shaken, he left the bomber and approached the copilot, who was standing at ease in a hangar, talking with his crew.

"Did you say that Captain Barton was speaking to you all the way from Frankfurt, giving you advice, helping you to fly and to land the B-twenty-four?" the surgeon asked.

"That's correct," the copilot acknowledged, frowning in bewilderment at the medico's strange question. "I told you that he talked me through my solo run from the time he was hit over Frankfurt until we landed. Why do you ask? You know Captain Barton. He never lets his men down. Sure, he was wounded, but he wouldn't let a little thing like a couple of bullet wounds slow him down."

"Yes, I know what a fine officer Captain Barton *was*," the

surgeon agreed "but you see, he died instantaneously when he was struck by those bullets. He couldn't have spoken to you from Frankfurt on. He would have been incapable of uttering any sound at all."

"What are you trying to tell me?" the copilot asked indignantly. "Are you telling me that Captain Barton has died? Are you saying that after getting us home safely, he died?"

The surgeon shook his head emphatically. "Captain Barton received mortal wounds over Frankfurt that killed him at once. I don't know *who* you heard talking to you or *who* guided your bomber home, but Captain Brick Barton has been dead for well over an hour!"

27. A Heavenly Helper Delivered a New Tire in Time of Dire Need

In the November 1967 issue of *Fate* magazine Marshall K. Mc-Clelland, who served as a correspondent for the GI newspaper *Stars and Stripes* during World War II, told of the time that he was with a group of four other journalists who had been cut off from U.S. armed forces and left to face a full-scale Japanese attack.

It all happened in the hills of Okinawa in May 1945. To what appeared to be their terminal dismay, the newsmen were stalled in a three-quarter-ton weapons carrier on the edge of a Japanese counterattack.

With McClelland were W. Eugene Smith, a well-known photographer affiliated with *Life* magazine; Harold Smith of the Chicago *Tribune*; Paige Abbott, a photographer for INP; and Lieutenant Bob Mitchell, public relations officer of the Seventh Infantry Division.

McClelland recalled that the men could do nothing other than sit helplessly in the crippled truck and await their fate. The weapons carrier had developed a flat tire, and the spare had been destroyed.

To make matters about as bad as they possibly could be, the five men were all alone—without even one friendly GI in sight. They were armed with one M-1 rifle, one carbine, and one .45 revolver among them.

And only a very short distance away, they could see a platoon of Japanese soldiers approaching the outskirts of the village where the journalists had been quartered.

Then, some thirty feet away near the edge of the road, Lieutenant Mitchell and Harold Smith simultaneously sighted a miracle: "a brand-new three-quarter-ton weapons carrier tire, full of air, mounted on a wheel, and ready to roll."

The journalists made good their escape just minutes before the deserted village suffered a terrible mortar bombardment and the Japanese took possession.

The mystery of just how the proper tire happened to materialize so near to them in their time of utmost need was never solved.

28. The Ghost of His Mother Saved Him from a Nazi Torpedo's Direct Hit

During World War II Victor Lasater of Omaha, Nebraska, had the misfortune to be temporarily stranded on a freighter in the middle of the Atlantic Ocean.

"Our engine had broken down about seven days out of port, and even though we were part of a convoy headed for Italy, the crucial war schedule demanded that the rest of the ships leave us behind while they went on," he remembered.

"In the period from 1942 to 1943 the waters of the Atlantic were thick with Nazi submarines, and they all had commanders eager to sink a ship for *der Führer*. We were all tense and nervous, expecting at any minute to see two or three of those terrible metal 'fish' streaking toward our helpless vessel."

By the third day of bobbing in the water like a sitting duck during hunting season, the crew was becoming really jumpy and tense.

"We had a few guns on deck," Lasater said, "but we all knew that they would be of little use against submarines unless the U-boat surfaced. And it was hardly likely that any Nazi commander, no matter how fanatical, was going to waste all that time and effort to surface in order to engage us in an old-fashioned sea battle when launching a couple of torpedoes at our ship from the safety of Neptune's domain would do the trick."

In late afternoon of the third day Lasater lay in his bunk, trying to get some rest before his next watch. He was alone in the quarters.

"I was awakened by the sensation that a warm hand was nudging my shoulder. I grunted and tried to shrug off the touch that was interfering with my sleep. But then, strangely enough, there seemed something very familiar about that particular style of nudging."

Lasater opened his eyes to see the image of his mother standing next to his bunk. She was still pushing at his shoulder, and when his eyes widened in astonishment at her presence, she smiled at him.

"Vic, honey," she told him in her softly pleasant voice, "you had better get up now. It is time to get up."

Before Lasater could respond, the form of his mother disappeared.

"Mom had been dead for eight years," he said. "I thought for a minute or so that maybe I had been dreaming, perhaps reliving a day in my childhood when my mother had been waking me to get ready to go to school.

"But the more I thought about the apparition, the more I began to feel so damn uneasy that I wanted to get dressed and get out of the bunk room as quickly as I could."

Since he did not wish to be alone and still had a couple of hours before he was to report to his watch, Victor Lasater decided to go down to the engine room and kibitz with the engineers who were working on the repairs.

"I had no more than nodded hello at one of the firemen who was a good buddy of mine when a tremendous explosion shook the entire freighter and knocked us all off kilter,"

Lasater said. "I went down on one knee, and a couple of the men fell flat on their backsides.

"No one had to tell us that we had been hit by a Nazi torpedo. One of Hitler's mighty U-boat commanders couldn't resist slamming one into a helpless freighter that was sitting dead in the water."

Within a matter of moments all of the crew members were crowded into lifeboats and rowing away from the sinking ship. Fortunately there were no casualties.

"But as I looked back at the slowly sinking freighter, I saw clearly that there would have been one fatality if the ghost of my mother had not awakened me when she did," Lasater said.

"From my position in the lifeboat I could see a massive hole that had been blasted in the starboard side where the torpedo had slammed us midship. Directly above that scorched and tangled mass of steel was the exact spot where I had been sleeping only moments before the torpedo had struck. My mother had somehow managed to go on recess from Heaven so that she would be able to wake me up just in time."

29. While He Evaded General Rommel's Afrika Korps, an Angel Brought Him Water in the Desert

A few years ago a man who had once served with the U.S. Rangers, an elite crack corps of rugged fighting men organized as a counterpart to the British commandos during the early days of World War II, told me a remarkable story which he swore was true. Since Mac was known as a businessman of high integrity and truthfulness in his community, it would seem that he would have little reason to muddy the facts surrounding the circumstances which saved his life.

As Mac told the story, he had become separated from his men after a vicious encounter with some brutally efficient members of General Rommel's Afrika Korps.

"They didn't call him the Desert Fox for nothing," Mac said. "Rommel was a brilliant strategist, a courageous officer, and his men were far from pussycats. They were tough, seasoned veterans, and it was our job to push them out of the African desert and knock them to their knees."

Battered from constant fighting and a bit the worse for wear, Mac knew that he had to keep going in the merciless heat and do his utmost to avoid walking right into the German Army and be killed or captured.

"I also knew that I had to go sparingly on the little bit of water that I had left in my canteen," Mac said. "But that scorching sun seemed to be sucking every drop of moisture from my body."

He knew that he was dehydrating quickly, and he did his best to conserve his energy. At the same time Mac realized that to remain stationary was absolutely no guarantee of survival with German patrols in the area.

"I had been in tight spots before," Mac said. "But I thought maybe this time my luck had run out. I figured someday some desert nomad would find my bleached bones drying in the sand."

When Mac was finally found several days later, his rescuers brought in a man in need of medical attention, but a man very much alive and not at all dehydrated. In fact, his canteen was still more than half full.

How had Mac survived? How could he possibly have lasted days in the desert on only a few sips of water?

Mac had a reputation among his men as being the toughest of the tough, always rugged and always ready, but nobody was that tough! No one could survive the broiling sun of the African desert without water. How could he have lasted on only half a canteen?

Although he is essentially an unchurched man, whose father was an avowed atheist, Mac said that he would tell his story of survival only to Father Tony, a Roman Catholic chaplain.

"An angel brought me water on the desert," Mac told the astonished clergyman. "Each day the angel would appear to me and fill my canteen with water. I could never have made it without that angel's help, Father. I guess I must not be all bad. I guess someone up there is looking out for me."

Mac had somehow managed to keep his canteen with him, and he handed it to the priest, sloshing it around as he did.

"See for yourself, Father Tony," Mac invited. "Take a drink of angel water."

Father Tony smiled and declined the offer, but having heard such remarkable testimony from so tough and no-nonsense a soldier as Mac, he was intrigued to the extent that he asked to have the water in Mac's canteen analyzed.

Later, he told Mac, the chemists had said that the water was extremely pure, that it contained *none* of the minerals or other substances which were indigenous to that area of the desert and of that region of Africa.

Father Tony was tempted to call it holy water.

And after he had survived the campaign in the African desert, the invasion of Italy, and the fall of Berlin, Mac returned home with the inspiration that he would help such young boys as those he saw orphaned by the terrible war. To this date he and his wife have served as foster parents to more than one hundred homeless boys.

As author Andrew Lang observed, "It is not only the imaginative or the ignorant or the unhealthy or the timid and nervous who report these abnormal experiences. If only school girls . . . or uneducated persons . . . or fools come forward with these tales, we might contemptuously reject them. But the witnesses are very often honorable men and women, brave, sane, healthy, not fanciful, not in a state of 'expectancy' (which, in fact, is usually fatal to ghost-seeing) and these persons have nothing to gain and some consideration to lose by reporting their experiences."

30. A Light Being Moved Them out of Harm's Way

A man, whom I shall call Bryan Peterson, told me of his remarkable experience in World War II when he firmly believes an angel saved his life and the lives of his buddies.

During the push to Berlin during the latter stages of the war Peterson and a group of his buddies were quartered in a brick farmhouse and told to get a good night's rest.

"The order was as unnecessary as telling a starving man to eat everything on his plate," Peterson said.

"We were all exhausted. Plus the fact that it had been raining for days, and this was the first time that we had had a roof over our heads in many a night."

The men finished a sparse but somehow comforting and filling meal.

"Even that GI mess tasted better with a fire going and a dry place to sleep that night," Peterson recalled.

"We had just begun to make ourselves really comfortable when a man carrying a bright light suddenly slammed open the door to the farmhouse and shouted, 'Everybody out! A mortar shell is about to hit!' "

Peterson and his buddies scrambled for the door, ran several yards from the farmhouse, then threw themselves headlong on the rain-soaked German soil.

Seconds later the demolished farmhouse was raining bricks down about them as Nazi mortar fire scored a direct hit on their very temporary sanctuary.

"It was a good thing for us that even though we were bone tired, we simply reacted on our training instincts," Peterson explained. "Logically how would *anyone* know in advance that a mortar shell was about to hit *any* specific target?

"What I mean to make clear is that the stranger did not burst into the farmhouse and shout, 'Heads up! The Jerries are going to start shelling this area!' He told us that a mortar shell was about to hit *our* house. Such a statement required special and specific knowledge that no one could have had.

"And who was the stranger? He wasn't an American soldier. He wasn't a German citizen warning us of an attack.

"The other thing is this: Later we all agreed that the man was not *carrying* a bright light; he *was* the bright light!"

Peterson said that a couple of days later, when the U.S. forces had advanced to a town where they were given a few hours for rest and relaxation, he and his buddies compared their memories of the remarkable event that had saved their lives.

"By that time we all agreed that the man had been surrounded by a brilliant kind of illumination," Peterson said. "I was convinced—and most of my buddies agreed—that an angel was responsible for having saved our lives that night."

31. The Mysterious Stranger Who Saved Clara Barton's Life

Clara Barton, founder of the American Red Cross, was a forty-year-old former schoolteacher when the Civil War broke out in 1861. As she perceived the opening weeks of what became the greatest and bloodiest carnage on United States soil, she saw a need for a system to distribute medical supplies and food to troops on the front lines.

After the war she worked tirelessly to establish an office that would help locate and identify prisoners, missing soldiers, and the dead who lay lost in unmarked graves throughout the North and the South.

Her doctors sent her abroad to Europe to rest and rejuvenate her state of exhaustion and ill health, and she arrived shortly before the outbreak of the Franco-Prussian War in 1870. She immediately began work with relief units of the International Committee of the Red Cross.

Forced into temporary retirement by the ill health that she had never taken the time to treat, she used her convalescence to begin lobbying the U.S. Senate to ratify the Geneva Convention and to establish an American Red Cross. In 1882 the

Senate managed to put aside its fear of foreign entanglements and the Geneva Convention was ratified, the American Red Cross was formed, and Clara Barton was named its first president.

It was in April 1884 that sixty-three-year-old Clara Barton, who had always professed to be a religious woman, met her guardian angel aboard the riverboat *Mattie Bell* on the Mississippi River.

A terrible spring flood had swept away corn and cotton fields, as well as homes and human lives, and Clara and a group of Red Cross workers were on a mission of mercy to bring food and medical supplies to the starving and the injured.

Before they set out, the captain of the *Mattie Bell* had warned her that it would be no pleasure cruise.

"We're going to be encountering floating trees, dead animals, and other debris—probably including human bodies," he said. "But the most dangerous threat to our mission will be submerged rocks and crevasses, waterfalls.

"You see, the flood has allowed the river to escape its former banks and to break through in new directions, and that means these crevasses can now be in places where they've never been before. I'll tell you straight, Miss Barton, a crevasse is a riverboat captain's worst nightmare."

Just as the *Mattie Bell* was about to push away from the dock, a Red Cross worker rushed up to Clara Barton with the report that a stranger had just stepped on board and was requesting permission to sail with them.

"Who is he?" she asked. "Is he a volunteer? If not, what is his business on this vessel?"

The worker told her that the stranger seemed rather vague

about his reasons for wanting to accompany them. "But Miss Barton, there is something, well, unusual about him."

"Unusual in what way?" Clara wished to know.

"I can't really say," the man admitted. "There's just *something* different about him."

Clara, always practical and direct, expressed her opinion that she saw no reason for a stranger, "unusual" or not, to accompany them. "Tell him that permission is denied," she told the Red Cross worker.

But the *Mattie Bell* was pulling away from the dock and the stranger was already on board. The captain had given the order to sail, and the assembled crowd of well-wishers was giving them a rousing sendoff, complete with a chorus of cheers and a band playing "The Battle Hymn of the Republic." The stranger was forgotten.

The captain had been right about the unpleasant sights that they would encounter. No member of the crew or the Red Cross workers could remain unmoved by the river currents carrying bobbing, swollen corpses of men, women, and children, as well as the carcasses of horses, cattle, cats, dogs, and other livestock and poultry. The Mississippi River had become a charnel house that moved inexorably toward New Orleans with its debris of death.

From time to time the captain would call out to Clara Barton, "Hear that roar? Just on the other side of that broken levee is a crevasse. Pray to God that we don't come on one of those hellholes unexpectedly."

It was nearly sundown when she recalled that they had a stranger in their midst. A worker pointed out the man standing alone at the stern, leaning on a railing, looking at the sunset.

"He seems an ordinary fellow," Clara remarked to her assistant. "And he does not appear to be bothering anyone. Nevertheless, when next we dock at a town, we'll put him ashore."

She had just made her decision about the stranger when the captain approached her with another matter that required her immediate response. "Miss Barton, I'm asking your permission to continue for a little while longer. There's a headland just a few miles farther on that would be an excellent spot to drop anchor for the night."

Clara was puzzled by the man's request. "Captain, the sun has nearly set. It was you yourself who sought to impress me with the many dangers inherent in this voyage. Wouldn't we be taking great risk by continuing after dark?"

The captain seemed to stiffen at her query. "You are, of course, nominally in command, so I must obey your orders. However, I was chosen for this voyage because of my great familiarity with the river. I am certain that I can make that headland before it becomes completely dark."

Clara reluctantly agreed to allow the captain to continue on toward the headland where he wished to anchor for the night.

"I suppose he's right," she said to her assistant. "A riverboat captain of his great experience should know what he's doing."

But then almost as if the demonic force of the flood had conspired to entrap the *Mattie Bell,* a thick fog seemed to appear from nowhere. Within moments the last rays of sunset had been swallowed up by the rolling clouds of fog, and the riverboat slowed to a crawl—far from the headland fancied by the captain.

As she had done in so many seemingly impossible and dangerous situations, Clara Barton gripped the cold railing of the ship and began to pray for God's help in seeing them through to safety.

A deep masculine voice startled her from her prayer. It was the stranger's voice, and although she could not clearly see his face in the darkness, she could hear plainly the urgency in his voice: "Within moments the steamboat will be in a crevasse, and it is a deadly one. The captain and engineer will not listen to me. You must command them to pull backward at once. If they do not, the ship will be lost—and all on board will perish!"

Clara Barton did not hesitate for even one second to argue the validity of the stranger's grim warning. There was something about his manner that precluded debate. She was immediately on her way to alert the captain of the danger.

Later she thanked God that the startled captain had not felt his authority threatened by a female. He had implemented her orders at once.

The crew and the Red Cross workers felt the *Mattie Bell* shudder to a stop. The rushing current of the crevasse could now be heard plainly by everyone.

To a person they all realized that their lives now depended on the little steamboat's reversed engines' being powerful enough to fight against the current that sought to pull them to their deaths.

To his credit, the captain displayed remarkable skill at the wheel as he managed to direct the *Mattie Bell,* groaning and creaking, engines shrieking, backward to an area where he felt secure in dropping anchor for the night.

At dawn's first light the men and women who had set out on a mission of mercy beheld with absolute horror the fate that a merciful God had spared them.

Immediately before them stretched a crevasse almost five hundred feet wide over which a torrent of rushing water dropped fifteen feet into the river below.

How had the stranger known of the existence of the broad and deadly crevasse?

Surely it had only recently been caused by the violent action of the floodwaters. The captain had not known of its ominous presence.

Without the stranger's warning they all would almost certainly have been killed by plunging into the crevasse.

Her eyes welling with tears and thankfulness, Clara Barton wished to commend the stranger for his action, which had saved the entire crew and the group of Red Cross workers.

"He's gone, Miss Barton," one of her staff told her. "He's nowhere on board the ship."

Clara frowned her bewilderment. "But that's impossible. He must be on board. Where else could he be? We're in the middle of a river made hazardous by floodwaters. Have you looked everywhere?"

The staff worker reminded Clara that the *Mattie Bell* was not a very large vessel. It did not take long to search out all of the places where a man might be sitting, standing, or resting.

The Red Cross worker who had first confronted the stranger when he had requested passage on the *Mattie Bell* reminded her that he had immediately noticed something different about him.

"I think he was an angel," the man said frankly, without embarrassment. "I think he came aboard solely for the purpose of seeing to it that our mission of mercy would not be terminated by a cruel, watery death."

Clara Barton nodded in silent agreement. She had always believed in angels, and she had always expressed her faith in God to work miracles. The Red Cross worker's explanation was good enough for her—and it seemed to satisfy the others on board the *Mattie Bell* as well.

Until her death in 1912 at the age of ninety-one, Clara remained unable to offer any "natural explanation" of who the stranger aboard the riverboat had been. If those with a skeptical or rational set of mind wished to devise other theories of how the man had known of the existence of the crevasse and how he had subsequently managed his complete disappearance from the *Mattie Bell,* she would not argue the case with them.

But she herself never wavered in her conviction that the unseen world had made itself manifest in order to protect the Red Cross workers on their humanitarian mission to the needy flood victims.

32. His Sick Wife Was Cured by Her Father's Ghost

After he had experienced a remarkable paranormal experience with what all his senses informed him had to be a ghost, the great British physicist and chemist Sir William Crookes still had trouble dealing with his suddenly enlarged universe. "Even now," he mused, "recalling the details of what I witnessed, there is an antagonism in my mind between reason, which pronounces [the ghost] to be scientifically impossible, and the consciousness, both of sense and sight, and these, corroborated, as they were, by the senses of all who were present—and not lying witnesses when they testify against my preconceptions."

When Sherry and I met with Howard Geary after we had conducted a workshop in Los Angeles in October 1992, he admitted to us that he, like Sir William Crookes, had been very much a product of the scientific age—and he had definitely been loaded with preconceptions about the "impossible reality" of ghosts and spirit guides.

"If anyone had told me a few years ago that I would be sitting in the front row of your seminar on angels, multidimensional beings, and ghosts, I would have told that person that he was completely nuts," Geary said, chuckling at his own reversal of prejudices.

According to Geary, he and his second wife, Virginia, had been married for only a few weeks in late August 1990 when she came down with a bad cough and a fever.

"It's my third day at work on this new job," she said, fighting back tears as she crawled into bed. "I've got to shake this nasty bug, honey. I can't afford to be sick right now."

Geary tried to soothe his bride's concerns. "You just worry about getting better. If you have to take a couple of days off, so be it."

By now the tears were moving unchecked over Virginia's cheeks. "That's easy for you to say, Howie. You've had your job for seven years. I've just started mine. I can't ask for sick leave after three days at work. They'll probably just decide to let me go."

"Bad things happen to good people," Geary said as he set a glass of water on the nightstand and shook two aspirin out of a bottle. "Here. Take these. And don't worry. You're good at your work, and your new bosses know it. They're not going to let you go because you caught a little flu bug."

Virginia shook her head at the proffered aspirin. "I've taken too many of those already. Oh, honey, this is no 'little flu bug.' I mean, I really got sick at the office. I had a coughing jag and nearly passed out.

"Someone felt my forehead and loudly announced to everyone within hearing distance—which was probably two blocks—that I had a raging fever. Pretty soon everyone was asking if I wanted them to call a doctor, an ambulance, a priest.

"I've wanted a job like this in advertising all of my adult

life. Now I've probably lost it on account of I have the bu-
bonic plague or something."

Geary knew how important the job seemed to be to Virginia, but he was helpless to do anything other than offer
moral support. She refused to go to a doctor for fear that she
might learn that she truly was ill with some disease or other,
so there seemed to be nothing to do until she asked for help.

The trouble was, Virginia appeared to be getting sicker by
the hour. She alternated between a high fever and chills, and
she seemed to have acute pains in her abdominal region.

Geary told us that he had set a deadline of midnight. If Virginia didn't seem better by then, he was carrying her off to the
emergency room at the hospital, regardless of her objections.

"I lay down on the couch so I wouldn't disturb Virginia,
and I flipped on television to watch one of the late-night talk
shows to pass the time," Geary said.

"The next thing I knew, I was jerking myself awake before
I slipped off the couch and fell to the floor. I had dozed off.
And my wristwatch was telling me that it was nearly two
o'clock. I had gone 'way past my deadline to decide whether
or not to take Virginia to the hospital."

Geary struggled wearily to his feet and was about to check
on Virginia in the bedroom when he had the eerie sensation
that they were not alone in their apartment.

"As I stood in the doorway of our bedroom, I was startled
to see a tall, heavyset man leaning over Virginia," Geary said.
"My heart started pounding, and I looked around for some
kind of weapon to defend us both against this very large burglar.

"But then I noticed that the big man had placed a hand
gently, lovingly on Virginia's forehead. By now I was really
confused. If this guy was a burglar, then he was the most affectionate one imaginable."

As if the intruder had suddenly become aware of Howard Geary's presence, he turned slowly and smiled at him.

"Although he had appeared as solid as a rock when I had first seen him," Geary said, "I was now able to see *through* him. He was becoming transparent right before my eyes. In spite of that, I could see clearly that he wore a bow tie and had on a three-piece suit. He was probably six feet four and about two hundred and fifty pounds.

"Just before he disappeared, he nodded at me, as if to say everything was going to be all right. A weird, luminous glow outlined his body, and he looked for a moment like the negative of a black-and-white photograph. Then he was gone."

Geary hastened to his wife's bedside. To his astonishment, she appeared to be sleeping peacefully.

He felt her forehead and neck, and amazingly, all traces of fever seemed to have left her.

"I didn't know what was going on," Geary said. "My mind was completely blown.

"I remember lying down beside Virginia to try to sort it all out. And then the next thing I knew it was morning, and I could hear that she was up early, cheerfully singing her version of selected rock and roll classics while she showered."

Bleary-eyed from lack of sleep, Geary fixed them both some coffee, orange juice, and toast. The peculiar events of the night before were still very jumbled in his groggy brain.

"Gee, honey," she said solicitously, gratefully accepting a cup of coffee from his shaking fingers, "you look terrible. Maybe you should stay home from work today."

"That's very funny." Geary forced a smile. "I had a really weird night last night—besides playing nurse to my ailing wife. Anyway, I'm really pleased that you experienced such a miraculous recovery."

Virginia nodded as she sipped at the hot coffee. "I had a wonderful dream that my father came to see me. When I was a little girl, Daddy was always so attentive to me when I was sick. He was an insurance salesman, but I told him that he should have been a doctor.

"You know, honey, he really had a true healing touch. Whenever he would put one of his big hands on my forehead, I would feel better right away. Didn't matter what was bothering me—stomachache, headache, measles, mumps—didn't matter at all. Daddy's touch could always make me feel better."

Intrigued, Geary asked his wife to describe her father. When she finished, he told her quietly that he had seen the image of a man who fitted that description in their bedroom at around two o'clock. He had seen the man put his hand on her forehead. And then he had disappeared. Like a ghost.

Virginia began to weep. She walked to a dresser, pulled out a small photo album, showed him a photograph of a tall, heavyset man holding a little girl. "Daddy and me," she said, her voice breaking. "I was five or six."

Geary nodded. It was unquestionably a picture of the ghostly gentleman that he had seen in their bedroom.

"Daddy died of a heart attack when I was only eleven," she told him. "I was with him when he died. We had just been running an errand to the supermarket for Mom. With his dying breath he told me that he would always be with me, and if I ever needed his help, he would be there.

"I loved him so much I was traumatized by his death. I didn't even speak for eight months after he died."

Geary took his wife into his arms and held her while she wept.

"I guess your father intends to keep his word never to leave you," he said gently. "Last night I saw him place his hand on your forehead and draw out the fever."

* * *

In concluding his fascinating account, Howard Geary told us that he was absolutely certain that he had not been dreaming when he saw the apparition of Virginia's father at her bedside. Then, of course, there was her miraculous recovery after the spirit's visitation.

"As I told you," he stated, "Virginia and I had been married for only a very brief time. It is the second marriage for both of us, and we had been seeing each for only six or seven months before we decided to get married. I knew that her mother lived back East in New Hampshire and that she had a brother somewhere in Michigan. She knew that my family was situated mostly in Colorado. We just hadn't had time to sort out relatives and so forth, so I had never even seen a picture of her father before I saw him that night in his etheric form.

"And now I'm hoping that he will visit again. He is obviously a very loving spirit."

33. The Doctor Came Back from the Dead to Save a Little Girl's Life

In his book *Encounters with the Unknown,* Colin Parsons relates an account of dramatic spiritual interaction when a mother's fervent prayers were somehow able to unlock the doors between worlds and summon miraculous assistance for her desperately ill little girl.

In September 1981 little Geraldine O'Rourke suddenly fell ill at the isolated rural home to which she had just moved with her parents. Helpless to prevent her condition from worsening, the O'Rourkes were dismayed when Geraldine's fever soon reached 101 degrees.

To make matters all the worse, the area was beset by a torrential downfall of rain, which prevented their taking her to a hospital, and their telephone was out of order, making a call for help impossible.

Just when the desperate parents' hopes were fast sinking in despair, Mrs. O'Rourke heard a peculiar rustling sound and looked up from her prayers to behold the figure of a man looking down at Geraldine on the bed. The mother felt no fear at the appearance of the phantom, and she immediately regarded the entity as one sent by God in answer to prayer.

The ghostly form led the amazed O'Rourkes to a hidden cache of medicines behind a panel in their living room. Trusting that the spirit entity had been sent by God to help them, they carefully followed the ghost's instructions regarding the proper administration of the medicines to their daughter.

As the astonished O'Rourkes watched, Geraldine became still and peaceful. The entity joined their vigil until dawn, then disappeared.

Later, after little Geraldine had fully recovered, the O'Rourkes did a bit of investigation and learned that their house had formerly been occupied by a doctor. Fearing that burglars would steal his drugs, he hid them in a secret compartment. But he had died so suddenly that he hadn't had time to leave instructions for their disposal.

The O'Rourkes will be forever grateful that the secret cache remained for the doctor's spirit to dispense to their daughter on that grim and stormy night. They have made a kind of shrine out of the compartment in which their helping hand from beyond had kept the medicines that saved Geraldine's life.

34. A Teenaged Ghost on a Motorcycle Changed Her Flat Tire So She Could Rush Her Child to the Hospital

On a hot, sticky August morning Colleen Granstrom of Huntsville, Alabama, was driving her three children to a park when one of her car tires blew on a remote rural section of road.

As she was struggling to maintain control of her automobile, Colleen's seven-year-old daughter, Holly, smashed her upper lip against the metal picnic basket that her older brother, ten-year-old Calvin, was clutching in his arms.

"When I thankfully managed to halt the car on a gravel shoulder of the road, I could see that Holly's lip was bleeding profusely," Colleen said. "I knew that it would require stitches."

"Momma!" Holly cried, holding her tiny fingers to her lip in a futile attempt to hold back the bleeding. "I'm going to bleed to death!"

"Gross!" Twelve-year-old Lynn pronounced in wide-eyed horror commingled with disgust from her position beside Colleen in the front seat. "Mother, I am about to be sick all over my new sundress!"

Colleen had never changed a flat tire in her life. Calvin valiantly helped her remove the jack and the spare tire from the trunk, but she was well aware that her young son had never even watched anyone change a flat.

"Calvin," she warned as he stumbled against a back door with the jack, "you're only going to hurt yourself!"

"But, Mom," he argued, "we've got to get Holly to a doctor. She is really bleeding bad!"

Colleen tried to calm herself by recalling the medical fact that head and scalp wounds always bleed heavily and appear worse than they are, but the fact remained that somehow she had to change the tire and get her baby to the emergency ward of a hospital.

Five . . . ten . . . fifteen minutes went by. There had been no cars on the desolate road to help them in that time. And there were no cars in sight.

The terrible humid August heat was doing its worst to make the situation even more unbearable. Lynn, yielding to compassion for her little sister, had forgotten about bloodstains on her new sundress and had crawled on to the backseat to hold a handkerchief to Holly's wounded lip. Holly was pale, trembling, and making tiny, frightened whimpering sounds.

Colleen was quickly approaching her panic level when a smiling young man on a motorcycle appeared and offered to help.

"I would really appreciate it," Colleen freely admitted. "My daughter is hurt and needs medical attention. And this heat just makes everything that much worse."

"No problem." Their rescuer smiled in an easy manner. Then, turning to Calvin, he winked and said, "You can hand me the tools when I ask for them."

The boy, who identified himself as Derek Kendall, worked

quickly, and he had the task completed in a matter of minutes.

"Wow, man," Calvin pronounced his admiration of the older boy, "you had that fixed in no time. And you didn't even break a sweat. How can you not sweat in this heat?"

Colleen offered Derek a cup of lemonade from their picnic thermos jug.

"Oh, no, thanks." Derek laughed. "Never touch the stuff!"

Colleen smiled at his joke. "It's only lemonade, Derek. You must be thirsty on such a hot day, riding your motorbike in the blazing sun and fixing flat tires for helpless ladies and kids in distress."

"I'm all right," Derek told her as he got on his motorbike. "You'd better hurry now and get Holly to a doctor."

Before he rode away, Derek refused Colleen's offer of money for his help, saying that he had no need of any "coin of the realm."

Later that night, however, after Holly had received stitches on her upper lip at the emergency room of the hospital and the Granstrom family was home safe and sound, Colleen and her husband, Charles, felt that it would only be right to send the lad a check for his trouble. They called information and got the listings for all the Kendalls in their area.

After a few calls Colleen was speaking to the mother of the teenaged good Samaritan, who broke into tears and asked her to describe the boy who had changed her tire.

Puzzled, Colleen obliged, right down to a description of the high school class ring Derek was wearing.

She felt the hairs stand up on her neck when the boy's mother informed her that Derek had been killed on that remote rural road just over a year before. He had been trying out the motorcycle that they had bought him for graduation.

Mrs. Kendall went on to state that her son had been a good boy who always derived pleasure from helping others.

Colleen could only express her sympathy and whisper around her tears that it would appear that Derek was somehow still helping people whenever he could.

35. The Ghost of a Caring Doctor Still Heals

Felicia Small of Jackson, Mississippi, received a distraught telephone call from her niece Judy Thorson just before eleven o'clock on February 12, 1986.

"Judy's six-year-old daughter, Carrie, had developed a fever that had gone sky-high, and her family doctor had decided to put her in the hospital," Felicia said. "Judy had called to ask if I could come down and sit with her. She had lost her husband in an automobile accident in 1984, and with her folks back in Chattanooga—she's my brother Rex's daughter—I was her only kin in the city."

When Felicia arrived at the hospital room that little Carrie shared with two other sick children, she was shocked to see how very ill she appeared.

"Lordy, Judy, why didn't you get that child to a doctor right away?" She scolded her niece. "That poor baby looks like death warmed over."

Judy, already red-eyed from crying and lack of sleep, told her aunt that she had done all that she had known to do.

"Carrie didn't take sick until around ten o'clock last night," she explained. "I sat up with her all night. Didn't get a wink of sleep myself. I must have sat in the doctor's office most of the morning, and he didn't put her in the hospital until this evening."

Felicia put comforting arms around her twenty-six-year-old niece. "Hush, hush, baby. It's all right. I'm sorry your cranky old auntie growled at you. I just don't want anything to happen to your baby."

Felicia sat with Judy for more than an hour before a heavy-set nurse with badly dyed red hair came in to check the other children in the room—who were both sleeping soundly—and to examine the desperately ill Carrie.

Both the girl's mother and great-aunt were disappointed with the cursory and mechanical treatment afforded by the bleary-eyed nurse, who appeared herself to be fatigued, drained, and hovering on the brink of illness.

"When will the doctor be by to check little Carrie?" Felicia asked politely.

"What doctor?" The nurse sniffed haughtily after first taking the time to blow her nose in a wad of tissue that she grabbed from Carrie's bedside stand. "If you see a doctor walking these corridors this time of night, you let me know. I'll want to alert the media so they can get it on the six o'clock news."

Felicia felt her cheeks redden with anger at the rude reply, but she controlled her emotions. "I was only asking because I am greatly concerned about the child's well-being."

The nurse softened one or two degrees. "Yeah, well, I'm sorry, but I'm all you've got until seven or eight in the morning."

After the abrasive nurse had left them alone, Judy hugged Felicia and cried into her shoulder. "I'm so glad that you're here with me."

"I'm afraid that all I can do is offer you some moral support, little girl." Felicia sighed. "It is apparent that the milk of human kindness in this hospital has curdled."

About ten minutes later an older nurse, who appeared to be in her fifties, stopped by to look in on Carrie, and her manner was in sharp contrast with the former nurse's cold indifference.

"She's such a pretty little girl." She smiled at Judy. "She looks just like her mommy. Don't you fret now, honey. She's going to be fine."

"But her fever seems so high," Judy said, fighting to hold back her tears. "I'm worried half out of my head."

"Isn't there some additional medication that can be prescribed to help the child through the crisis point?" Felicia asked.

The kind woman shook her head as her fingers gently brushed a moist strand of hair away from Carrie's eyes.

"You know that we nurses are not allowed to prescribe any medication," she answered in a soft, almost musical voice.

"But *you know* that she needs some additional medication, don't you?" Felicia's voice rose to a plea, rather than a demand.

When the nurse turned her attention back to the women, they could see that tears had begun to form in her eyes. "I'm Nurse Elms. If there is anything I can do, please call me. The nurses' station is just down the hallway."

"Well"—Felicia sighed, dropping her arms helplessly to her side after Nurse Elms had left the room—"we still don't have any help for poor Carrie, but at least we've seen that human decency in this hospital still manages to stay alive in the body of that dear woman."

Both Felicia and Judy were dozing when a tall, youthful doctor in a navy blue three-piece suit walked into the room just a few minutes after two in the morning. He went directly to the foot of Carrie's bed, picked up her chart, and scanned it quickly.

"Yes, yes, my, my, hmm," he mumbled to himself. The way he twitched his mustache as he read the medical staff's notations reminded Felicia of a large rabbit.

He turned to face the women, as if noticing them for the first time. He appeared to be in his mid to late thirties, and his smile was broad and friendly. When he spoke, his voice was deep, rich, and confident.

"She's a pretty sick little girl. There's no doubt about that," he admitted. "But don't you worry. I have just the magic brew that will fix her up in no time."

"Thank you," Judy said, squeezing her aunt's hand in relief and joy. "Thank you, Dr.—"

"I'm Dr. Vanbuhler, ma'am. And there's no need to thank me. I'm just doing my job, don't you know."

Felicia began to relax for the first time since Judy's telephone call. "Well, I wish there were more people like you doing their job around this hospital," she said to the doctor as he readied a syringe for an injection in Carrie's bottom.

"Yes, yes." Dr. Vanbuhler nodded. "It is a shame, isn't it?"

"If only some of the other staff members would love their work as much as you appear to," Felicia said.

"There is no question that I truly do love my work," he agreed, then mumbled a bit more before he began to whistle some nondescript tune that sounded like his personal rendition of circus or parade music.

The cheery doctor finished giving Carrie an injection, gave her an affectionate pat on the bottom, and left the room after a hurried but courtly bow to Judy and Felicia.

"Now that's the doctor that I'm requesting if I am ever a patient in this hospital." Felicia laughed.

* * *

At five-thirty Carrie sat up and asked for a drink of water.

Felicia stroked the child's forehead while Judy went to get Nurse Elms. To her layperson's hands, it seemed as though Carrie's fever had left her.

Within minutes a beaming Nurse Elms had verified Felicia's diagnosis with a thermometer.

When Carrie's physician, Dr. Watney, arrived at seven, he carefully examined the girl and said that he was pleased to declare that her fever was gone.

"Let's just keep her until late-afternoon discharge time, though," he said to Judy. "We want to be certain before we send her home."

Felicia reached for her coat and purse. "Unless you need me for anything, hon," she said to Judy, "I guess I'll go on home. Praise God for Dr. Vanbuhler."

Dr. Watney looked up from the notepad on which he was writing and frowned quizzically. "Who is Dr. Vanbuhler?"

Felicia shrugged. "I guess he's the doctor on the late late shift around here."

"There is no Dr. Vanbuhler on staff, and there is no doctor on duty here after ten o'clock." Dr. Watney's smile had disappeared, and his amiable bedside manner was beginning to fade away into thinly veiled annoyance.

"Judy," he demanded of his patient's mother, "does your aunt have a peculiar sense of humor?"

"Why, no, Dr. Watney." Judy protested his insinuation. "Dr. Vanbuhler stopped by the room around two last night and gave Carrie a shot. I'm pretty sure that it was that shot that made her better."

Dr. Watney's cheeks were becoming very red. "No one authorized any kind of injection for Carrie."

His impatient fingers flipped the pages of Carrie's medical chart. "And there is absolutely no notation to indicate that she had any kind of injection or any medication other than that which I authorized."

Judy's glare defused any full-blown outburst from the doctor, and her voice was steady, measured, free of doubt: "We saw him. He was here. He gave Carrie a shot."

"Very well, then," he said, pushing the button near Carrie's pillow that would summon a nurse. "We'll just get to the bottom of this at once. I will not have anyone in this hospital giving unauthorized medication to any of my patients."

"The cold and indifferent heavyset nurse, who truly appeared on the verge of collapse, together with our loving Nurse Elms, agreed with the stern-faced Dr. Watney that there was no Dr. Vanbuhler on the staff and that Carrie had received no injection of any kind during the night," Felicia said.

"There was something about Nurse Elms's demeanor that caused both Judy and me to drop the matter and say that we must have dozed off and imagined the whole episode in some kind of dream. Dr. Watney seemed relieved with such a silly explanation, and it was obvious that he just wanted to get on with his daily rounds."

A few minutes later, as Felicia was walking across the hospital parking lot toward her car, Nurse Elms caught up with her.

"I just want you two nice ladies to know that you aren't crazy or anything," she said. "You aren't the first ones that Dr. Vanbuhler has helped, but generally I get to them first so they don't say anything to any of the doctors on staff."

Felicia frowned and asked nervously if Dr. Vanbuhler was some kind of maverick M.D.

"No." Nurse Elms smiled. "Nothing like that. You see, Dr. Vanbuhler has been dead for nearly thirty years. A youngster like Dr. Watney would never have heard of him."

Felicia has always been open toward accounts of the paranormal, so she encouraged Nurse Elms to tell her more about the ghostly physician.

"He was truly a wonderful, caring doctor," Nurse Elms said. "He was on staff when I first came to work here. I was only nineteen. Dr. Vanbuhler was in his mid-thirties, and I thought he was what an ideal physician should be. He was completely devoted to the healing arts and to helping his patients.

"Sometimes it is really difficult to understand God's ways, but that saintly young doctor was killed in the hospital late one night by a teenaged mental patient who had got hold of a scalpel and in his delusion thought Dr. Vanbuhler was the father who had abused him.

"I've seen his ghost walking the corridors of the hospital on three or four occasions," she concluded. "I think his spirit is given some kind of life force by his desire to help the sick. And every so often, as in the case of your niece's child, he manifests in physical form to continue his healing work. In my book, even though he's a ghost, he's still my ideal of what doctors should be."

36. The Spirit Doctor Who Healed from Beyond the Grave—and Even Treated Two U.S. Presidents

The warming glow of morning sunlight cast an orangish haze over Marion County, Virginia, on the morning of March 15, 1852. In the home of Phillip and Sarah Bannock a black-clad midwife had worked desperately through the night to ease Mrs. Bannock's intense labor pains. As if her responsibilities to the suffering mother were not enough in themselves, the midwife had been hampered in her work on several occasions by Phillip Bannock, a deeply religious man, who prayed fervently for a son.

When a sharp slap sounded at last from the back bedroom, Bannock ran toward the lusty squalls from the newborn babe.

The midwife hesitated to reveal the sex of the child when she saw the wild-eyed husband come storming into the room. Remaining solicitous to the comfort and needs of the exhausted mother, she ignored the entreaties of Phillip Bannock as long as she could before she told him, "Mother and child are both doing well, sir. You have a beautiful daughter."

"A . . . daughter," Bannock echoed hollowly, as if he were

repeating a pronouncement of sadness rather than an announcement of joy.

The ashen-faced father drew closer, making no effort to conceal his disappointment or to offer assurances of love to his wife, who lay smiling feebly, her hair and bedclothes soaked with sweat.

"What—what is that on the child's face?" he asked the midwife.

"It's a veil of mucus," the woman explained as she set about cleaning the baby and wiping her wrinkled face before handing her over to her mother. "There are those folks who declare that those babies born with a veil over their face will be blessed with prophetic powers."

"Then it is the mark of the devil!" Bannock gasped, drawing back from his newborn daughter. "She is a child of darkness. I will have nothing to do with the devil's daughter."

The midwife glared at him. "You may be a deacon in the church and all"—she sighed in disgust—"but I'll tell you, Phillip Bannock, that your brand of religion is too prejudiced for the likes of me."

Maude Bannock grew into a dark-haired, bright-eyed child in spite of the cold rejection by her father. When she was an infant asleep in her crib, Phillip Bannock would look in on her and swear that he saw weird lights floating around her slumbering form. Later he told those wide-eyed members of his congregation who bothered to listen to him that he had observed electric sparks fly from the little girl's fingertips.

One day when Maude was approaching six years of age, she was in the family kitchen watching her mother brew a large tub of lye water for the family washing. Her mother left the kitchen for just a moment, but it was long enough for the child to tip the vessel of boiling lye water and to scald herself.

After Dr. Edson Woodruff, the local physician, had examined Maude, he told the anxious mother that the little girl had second- and third-degree burns over most of her body. "I can't give you much hope for her recovery," he said soberly.

Each morning for five consecutive days Dr. Woodruff rode to the Bannock home and did what he could for the child.

On the sixth morning of his conscientious visits the general practitioner was applying a poultice to the burns when the tiny girl's body stirred. Although her eyes remained closed and for all appearances she was still unconscious, she grabbed a pencil from the doctor's pocket and began to mumble feebly in a weak voice.

"She seems to want a piece of paper," said the mystified doctor as he laid a prescription pad in his little patient's lap.

"What would she want with paper and pencil?" Phillip Bannock growled impatiently. "She can't read or write."

Dr. Woodruff acknowledged Bannock's argument with a brief nod, but he watched incredulously as little Maude wrote: "Obtain a large basket of pine needles and crush them. Mix with linseed oil. Put between beet leaves. Apply immediately."

When Bannock saw the writing for himself, he pronounced the script as but another example of his daughter's devil work.

"I tell you that Maude has not been schooled. She doesn't know how to write. It is Satan working through her!"

Dr. Woodruff became visibly shaken as he quietly studied the writing on the pad. "I know this handwriting," he said. "It is that of Dr. DeHaven, a physician who once practiced with me in another city. That blessed gentleman has been dead for many years now, but somehow, through the grace of God, he has just written a prescription that may well help me to heal this child."

Bannock's face became red and swollen with rage and fear. "Are you saying that a dead man, a restless spirit, has possessed our daughter?"

Mrs. Bannock began to weep and to tremble as she sank weakly into a chair near the fireplace.

"I knew the moment that Maude was born that she belonged to the devil," Bannock fulminated.

"Bosh!" Dr. Woodruff scolded the ranting father of his patient. "Say rather that an angel from Heaven has summoned my old friend with all of his vast medical knowledge to manifest to help Maude become well. Why is it that you people are always so ready to give credit for so many wonderful things to the devil? I like to believe that it is God and his marvelous, caring angels that help me to heal my patients."

"The doctor is right, Phillip." Mrs. Bannock spoke up. "Let us pray to the holy ministering angels for Maude's recovery rather than give power to the devil."

In spite of her father's objections, the prescription from beyond the grave was administered to the blistered body of little Maude Bannock. Although she was troubled by aftereffects of the burns for many years, the crisis passed, and she recovered from the accidental scalding.

However, the tutelary spirit of Dr. DeHaven remained always with her. Years later, in the latter part of the nineteenth century, as Maude Lord-Drake, she became famous as one of the nation's most gifted clairvoyants, spiritualist mediums, and healers.

Under the control and the guidance of Dr. DeHaven's spirit, Maude, the child cursed by her father as the devil's daughter, treated thousands of desperately ill patients. On numerous occasions dozens of orthodox medical doctors witnessed these phenomenal healing sessions and even signed affidavits attesting to the powers of Maude Lord-Drake's therapeutic séances.

In addition to scores of ordinary men and women across the continent, such prominent Americans as President Chester A. Arthur, President Ulysses S. Grant, manufacturer George

Pullman, and philanthropist Leland Stanford, who established Stanford University in California, were among those who received healing comfort from Dr. DeHaven, the benefactor from beyond who manifested through the physical vehicle of Maude Lord-Drake.

37. The Ghost of Pope John XXIII Cured a Dying Nun

Early in 1967 the *Irish Independent* of Dublin carried the account of a miracle healing that had brought a dying nun "from death's door to a healthy normal life after Pope John appeared and spoke to her."

Sister Caterina Capitani, a nun of the Sisters of Charity of St. Vincent de Paul, suffered from varicose veins of the esophagus, a condition thought to be incurable and surgically inoperable. However, because the unfortunate sister endured continual hemorrhages, physicians decided to attempt an operation at Medical Missionaries of Mary of the Clinica Mediterranea in Naples, Italy.

Two surgeries were performed, but they were unsuccessful, and when the incision on her stomach opened, Sister Caterina's condition steadily worsened to the point where she collapsed.

Desperate to attempt any new therapy, her doctors sent the nun south for a change of air, but she was soon returned to Naples when it was decided that she was dying. The Medical Missionaries had no bed immediately available when she arrived, so Sister Caterina was taken to a nearby hospital.

The next day, when they had suitable accommodations for the nun, the Medical Missionaries were advised that it would be useless to move Sister Caterina, as she was dying and had only a very brief time to live.

"I was all alone," Sister Caterina recalled. "I had been turned on my side and left alone.

"Then I felt somebody place a hand on my stomach. Summoning all my strength, I turned to see Pope John standing beside my bed. He was not in his papal robes, but I recognized him easily."

In a quiet yet authoritative voice, the ethereal image of Pope John XXIII, who had died on June 3, 1963, spoke words of great comfort: "Sister, you have called to me so many times, as have so many of the Sisters of Charity of St. Vincent de Paul, that you have torn out of my heart this miracle. But now do not fear. You are healed!"

The spirit of Pope John then told Sister Caterina to call in the sisters and the doctors so that a test could be made.

"But first he assured me once again that no trace of my illness would remain," Sister Caterina said. "Just before he vanished, he told me, 'Come to Rome and pray at my tomb. I await you.'"

The moment the ghost of the deceased pope disappeared, Sister Caterina rose from her bed and was elated that she felt no pain.

When she summoned the sisters and doctors into her room, they were amazed to find that the scar on her abdomen, which had been open and bleeding, was now completely healed. There was, in fact, no longer any scar or any other physical sign to indicate that moments before, there had been a gaping wound.

"It is a miracle," one of the sisters remarked. "Sister Caterina was not expected to survive the day, yet that evening she was up and eating her supper with the community."

According to the *Irish Independent,* the miracle healing of Sister Caterina by the ghost of Pope John XXIII occurred in May 1966. "Ever since," the account reads, "the nun has lived a healthy life. This is a phenomenon that cannot be explained in a human way."

Psychic News, the well-known British spiritualist weekly, agreed that the miraculous healing was a splendid event that could not be "explained in a human way," but it could not resist musing that when such an intervention of spirit entities occurred among the orthodox clergy, it was regarded as a miracle. On the other hand, whenever similar phenomena occurred among members of spiritualist groups, the papacy would be likely to denounce the "miracle" as the "work of the devil."

To be fair, it should be acknowledged that most claims of "miracles" are not sanctioned or authenticated by the Roman Catholic Church with unquestioning acceptance.

For instance, if a devout parishioner were to tell his priest that an angel had appeared over his sickbed and healed him, the clergyman would probably express his joy over the man's miraculous healing. However, if another member of the parish should question the priest and ask pointedly if it truly were a miracle that had cured his friend, the priest might smile and answer by saying, "If you believe, no proof is necessary. If you don't believe, no proof is sufficient."

However, if our recipient of the miracle cure should begin to offer his former sickbed as a shrine for other pilgrims seeking instantaneous healings and if subsequent claims of "miracle healings" should begin to disrupt parish life, then the Catholic Church would initiate an investigation of the validity of the parishioner's alleged miracle. The investigative process would begin with the local bishop, who would convene a committee of experts who would proceed to examine theological, scientific, or personal circumstances surrounding the claims for the miracle.

Father Frederick Jelly, professor of systematic theology at Mount St. Mary's Seminary in Emmitsburg, Maryland, a veteran of service on miracles committees, listed for the Gannett News Service the principal criteria by which a miracle would be evaluated (May 14, 1993):

- What is the psychological state of the person claiming the miracle?
- Is there a profit motive behind the miracle claim?
- What is the character of the person who claims the miracle?
- What are the spiritual fruits of the miracle? Does it attract people to prayer, greater acts of charity, and so forth?

If the miracles committee should decide that an event is miraculous, the case may be referred to the Vatican's Sacred Congregation for the Doctrine of the Faith in Rome, which can inaugurate a new investigation or pass along its recommendation for acceptance to the pope, the final arbiter of miracles for the Roman Catholic Church.

As a phenomenologist, one who researches and reports such remarkable occurrences, I must question whether Sister Caterina's spirit healer was truly that of Pope John XXIII or if a benevolent entity had merely chosen that guise in order to accomplish a more effective healing miracle. In either event, a devout nun was delivered from the valley of death by "someone" up there who definitely liked her.

38. Someone "Down There" Doesn't Like Us at All!

I have had the privilege and the very good fortune to have met or to have corresponded with so many of the heroes of my childhood and youth, and high on the list would be the author-screenwriter and psychic-sensitive extraordinary Harold Sherman. Harold and I shared the lecture platform on numerous occasions before his recent passing, and I shall cherish the memory of the times that we engaged in delightful and insightful conversations that lasted for many hours at a session.

Even such a highly spiritual individual as Harold Sherman encountered the evil interlopers of the astral world who masquerade as angels of light and who are always at the ready to deceive the gullible and the unwary. He became extremely cautious in his advice to the many men and women who sought his counsel, and he emphasized serious study and self-discipline over careless experimentation with the occult and with processes of pseudomagic that sought to invoke angels and entities to do one's bidding.

Harold came to international attention in 1937, when the

Russian aviator Sigismund Levanevsky and his five crew members vanished while on a daring flight over the polar regions. The Soviet government prevailed upon the well-known British Arctic explorer Sir Hubert Wilkins to conduct a search for the missing airmen.

Just before Sir Hubert was to leave on his mission on October 15, 1937, he had lunch with Harold, and the two men agreed to attempt to remain in contact with each other by telepathy during the days of the search—specifically from eleven-thirty to midnight on Monday, Tuesday, and Thursday evenings. At those times the two men would concentrate on their achieving telepathic rapport, and Sir Hubert would try to "transmit" precise information concerning the position and progress of the expedition.

At each of the sessions Harold retired to his study and darkened all the lights before sitting in a chair facing a blank wall. He kept a pad, a pencil, and a flashlight at his side.

As he began concentrating, he almost immediately began receiving a series of vivid yet very confused images of what appeared to be the Arctic. Since the purpose of the experiment was to receive intelligible information through telepathy, Harold focused upon a mental picture of Sir Hubert until, by the force of his will, the maze of images congealed into one.

In the final analysis the information conveyed by Harold Sherman about the progress of Sir Hubert's expedition may not have been as precise as a formal report might have been, but the psychic's impressions were surprisingly accurate. Harold had been able to determine the location of the expedition, the events which Sir Hubert observed, and the mechanical difficulties that the explorer was having with the plane that he flew.

Reginald Iverson, who had been hired by the *New York Times* to keep in radio contact with the search expedition, found that sunspot and magnetic conditions had made regular communication impossible, and he had been able to get through to Sir Hubert on only a very few occasions. In an affidavit, which Iverson signed after the unsuccessful search for the Russian fliers had been completed, he testified that Harold Sherman had been able to receive more accurate knowledge via telepathy with Sir Hubert than he had been able to gain from his sporadic radio contact with the expedition.

For the rest of his long and fruitful life Harold Sherman devoted his energies toward helping ordinary men and women with the same mental powers that had enabled him to maintain telepathic contact with an Arctic explorer halfway around the world.

Some years ago Harold undertook the monumental task of freeing a woman from the influence of an evil entity that had sought to take possession of her after she had begun experimenting with automatic writing. According to the woman, to whom he gave the name of Edna, she had sought a guardian angel and instead had received an "astral tramp," who posed as a spiritual adviser, guardian angel, and guru. Edna bemoaned the fact that she had fallen for the whole thing because she had not realized that such evil entities existed.

"He has followed me, bugged and badgered me for a whole year," Edna told Harold. "He has kept me awake nights with his dirty, filthy, perverted sex talk and mental pictures.

"How do I get rid of this thing? I've spent hundreds of dollars on pills and doctors. Last night, he said, 'Kill the kids, Edna!' over and over again."

Harold replied to Edna's desperate letter at once, seeking frank and honest answers to some questions and reminding her that he had always warned the readers of his many books that one should not get involved with automatic writing because there were evil as well as good forces that might seek to make attunement with an open and receptive human mind.

In her return correspondence to Harold, Edna insisted that she had never read any material of a pornographic nature. She was a regular churchgoer and read primarily works of an inspirational nature. It had only been her religious faith that had sustained her during this awful period of demonic to

re   ature is very
re   first, and af-
te   irt and filth."
a   d Edna with
a   ffending en-
tit   as a kind of
sp   ers who had
fo   'Get out and
sta   nytime, any-
w   ow you out.
Yo

pe   he might re-
pe   e had devel-
op   orce within.
In

I am never alone, God . . . is always with me. . . .

I am part of God, and God has a great purpose in life for me which He is revealing day by day as I grow in strength of body, mind, and spirit.

. . . I have the power to overcome all things within me.

In God's care, no harm can befall me.

I now give myself over to God's protection, and I will follow His guidance day by day.

In the mid-1970s I corresponded with Gloria, a woman from Tennessee, who had also found herself ensnared with one of the "astral tramps" that assume the guise of angels in order to seduce and deceive their human victims. She was fortunate enough to have undergone an awakening process with her true guardian spirit that managed to free her from the malevolent being that had deceived her.

Gloria's first extrasensory experience occurred in 1963, when she traveled astrally.

"I stood at my bedroom window and 'saw' through walls. It was a few moments before I realized that my body was still asleep on the bed."

She had never before heard of such things. "I was so amazed that I told everyone I could capture for an audience, hoping that someone could explain it to me. They either looked at me with fright or dismissed it as a dream."

But Gloria's search for answers had been set in motion. Cautiously, at first, because of her strict Baptist upbringing, she began to read some books on metaphysics and to practice meditation.

Then *someone* began to flash back the answers to her mental questions.

"Before long this *someone* had taken on a personality. He was my image of the Ideal. He was infinitely patient and possessed of keen yet compassionate humor."

When her husband, who was in the military service, sent for her to join him in his overseas assignment, Gloria's "Companion" became more vivid, and her general feeling of well-being greatly increased. Minor illnesses were cured overnight, and she was flooded with energy to accomplish whatever goal she wished to achieve.

By the time she and her husband returned to the United States, Gloria had discovered the Ouija board, and she now believed herself to be completely awakened.

"It seemed to me that my Companion was taking a more active role in my life and that he was encouraging me to explore the deeper mysteries of the universe. He told me to seek out certain occult practices and to try my hand at them.

"My consciousness leaped ahead in time, speeding, out of control. I saw other dimensions and the creatures in them. I understood their needs, their problems. I felt their misery, as well as their joy. Many times I was visited by astral forms. I even became aware of the 'children' in the astral world who were my 'students.'

"At the same time I was working a full-time job in the objective world and doing it without asking my Companion for additional strength. I was filled with incredible energy, and I felt my guide urging me on to explore even further into the in-between dimensions. Sleep didn't matter. Food didn't matter. My family didn't matter. What did matter was exploring the astral worlds."

Eventually, however, Gloria's hold on the material world began to slip.

"The two dimensions became one—with my consent, of course. I felt that I had the ability to bring the subjective and objective worlds into focus, thus giving deeper meaning to both."

Gloria's daughter began to work the Ouija board with her. "But her two dimensions never overlapped. Her objective life stayed objective. She had some inner protection that kept her free from distortion. She is the strongest person spiritually I know."

When her daughter withdrew from working the board with her, Gloria no longer had the younger woman's natural objectivity to ground her.

"The Gateway between dimensions broadened, and I could no longer control the entities who chose to traffic between dimensions. For a period of a week entities forced themselves through and tried to possess my husband and my son through me."

As she fell into greater mental and spiritual confusion, she became more aware of the true identity of the being that had been responsible for directing her mad whirl through other dimensions. This being had assumed the role of her spiritual companion, her guardian, and had deceived her into going on her psychic power trip.

"He seemed malevolent, and he took great satisfaction in having forced me to play his game. He taunted me and said that I was in his power and must now obey his every command.

"I tried to reject him, pitting my will against his. In spite of all my energy being directed against him, he grew stronger and I grew more exhausted."

At the moment when she thought she would surely perish, Gloria called out for her true companion, her true guardian spirit.

"He manifested and dissolved the blackness around me. Knowledge of my complete Self returned to me, and I knew what the blackness was and who the malevolent entity was. It was myself, my lower self, the self that contained all the negativity that I had ever collected.

"And then my spirit guide set me free to float in a timelessness in which there was no past, present, or future. There was nothing to press me or make demands of me. I was my Original Self—before life and after life.

"I called out into the darkness, and out of nothing came a magnificent light, my Companion, my guide; and I realized that he had never really left me during my experience with the malevolent being that had manipulated my lower self.

"In the years since my awakening, I know how to 'run with the world,' though I will never again be caught up in it," Gloria said. "I know that my true spiritual guide is there for me, and my requests are very small. I once again love life, and I am once again playing the game—but this time with guidance."

39. The Hex of the Horrible Cupid

My Indonesian friend Jannes Lumbantobing is from a village on Samosir, an island in the middle of Lake Toba in Sumatra, Indonesia. We became good friends many years ago, and when we last visited, he was a guest in our Iowa home on a three-day stopover before he entered a seminary. He had converted to Christianity some years before, and now he believed that he had experienced a call to serve his people in the capacity of a pastor.

Although Jannes (who always preferred that I call him Jim) believed firmly in the existence of ministering angels of God, he had also seen the angels of darkness at work performing their painful enterprises against human beings.

"Christianity has brought many changes to my native Indonesia," Jim said as we relaxed with a soft drink in my study. "But in the outlying *angka huta* [villages], the old beliefs remain strong. Here the villagers may give lip service to the Christian God, but *mamele* [worship] of the old gods is observed with fervor.

"Although you are a student of such things, Brad, you will

agree that much of what I have shared with you in our many conversations over the years would be difficult for most Americans to believe. They live in the United States with their fast cars and their concrete highways. They believe themselves to be completely removed from the primitive and elemental. It is only in certain terrifying situations that Americans may be reminded that the dark powers are very potent. And if they should ever visit the environment of remote villages in Indonesia, Africa, South America, or Asia, they would observe a power of evil that can become formidable in the extreme."

When Jim was a teenager in his village, he witnessed a not uncommon phenomenon: The ugliest boy in his high school class fell in love with the prettiest girl.

What followed, however, would be judged very uncommon by most Western standards.

The boy began to court the young beauty and, quite understandably, was instantly rebuffed. The young man could hardly count on his good looks or his personal magnetism to help him out with the haughty object of his affections. But he had another advantage that transcended any and all physical properties: He was the nephew of the *datu,* the village witch doctor.

One day, during a study period at school, Jim noticed the rejected suitor stretch across his desk to pluck unnoticed a few loose hairs that lay on the shoulders of the desired girl's blouse.

At that time young Jim had no idea why the frustrated lover boy would settle for some hairs from her head when he seemed to want the whole person. Jim didn't yet have the faintest idea about such things as sympathetic or mimetic magic.

It wasn't until the conclusion of the series of strange events that had been set in motion by this simple act that Jim was made aware of such terrible projects of evil as shaping a figure in the likeness of one whom the *datu* wished to harm by hexing.

Jim was to learn that the effectiveness of the magic required strands of hair, nail clippings, blood—something that would form an unbreakable bond between the pretty young victim and the demons, the evil spirits, the angels of darkness, that had been set upon her.

But at that stage of his spiritual knowledge Jim was surprised when the girl was absent from school the next day.

Later, during the evening meal, Jim's father told him that the girl lay in a coma, unable to take either food or drink. She was asleep yet not asleep. Her eyes were open wide, unblinking. Over and over again she repeated only one word: the name of the *datu's* nephew.

Within a week the girl was emaciated. She had eaten nothing, and she had drunk only the few drops of water that her distraught parents had managed to force down her parched throat.

The medical missionaries were helpless. Their Western medicines had no effect upon the hex. The girl became even worse after their visits. It was as if the creatures of darkness resented the ineffectual meddlings of another culture and took out their wrath upon the tormented body of the young girl.

In desperation the distressed father of the girl sought aid from three *datus* in a nearby village, but after taking his money and performing a number of worthless rituals and chants, the trio of witch doctors admitted that they were powerless to drive back the demons that had been set loose to torment the man's daughter.

The father could no longer avoid the inevitable confrontation with the *datu* of his own village, the very one who had set the horrid things of darkness upon his beloved daughter.

The *datu* remained impassive to the desperate man's pleas. The fact that his daughter had been reduced to a hollow-eyed, babbling wretch was, he told the father, no concern of his.

The man fell to his knees and promised to give the *datu* what little wealth he had left.

At last the witch doctor, who had been feigning indifference, agreed to intercede for the man's daughter and to negotiate with the evil spirits that had taken up residence within her frail body.

Within a week the girl was smiling weakly in her mother's arms and calling feebly for rice and water.

However, it wasn't until the young girl had completely recovered from her mysterious delirium that the *datu* and his triumphantly grinning nephew arrived at her home.

"My nephew," the witch doctor said, indicating the ugly, hulking young man at his heels, "desires to marry your daughter."

The girl's parents were indignant and outraged by the *datu's* words—even though they had not been unexpected.

"Never," replied the father, shaking his head emphatically. "My daughter is lovely and sweet-voiced. She can have the pick of any wealthy young men in the village."

The *datu's* eyes narrowed. "Ah, my friend, but she was not so lovely and sweet-voiced when you came begging to me on your knees for her very life. It would be a pity if the fever were to return."

The threat was obvious. The insinuation did not need to be stated any more clearly or elaborately. The *datu* had hexed the lovely girl once, and he was unhesitatingly prepared to work his evil on her again if need be.

The father stammered, his fists opening and closing in helpless rage. His wealth was depleted from the expense of the three unsuccessful *datus* in the neighboring village. And no one seemed able to combat the evil spirits that awaited the confident witch doctor's bidding. He knew that he had no choice. Although he was repelled by the very thought, he must give his daughter to the *datu*'s nephew to be his bride.

"The *datu* had saved his daughter's life," Jim explained. "According to Batak custom, one owes his life to someone who has helped him. There was nothing for the father to do but to accept the nephew's marriage proposal. The beautiful girl had to go through with the marriage or die.

"So you see, Brad," Jim concluded, "it truly is as you have so often said and written: Whether in the United States or among the Batak, one must be wary of all manifestations of the dark angels and pray for protection from all evil spirits."

40. Creating the Proper Attitude Toward the Concept of a Spirit Guide or a Spirit Teacher

As I emphasized in an earlier chapter, messengers and guides from a Higher Intelligence are sent, not summoned.

I very much believe, as the Native American Medicine priests instruct their students, that a spirit that is called by us and asked to do our bidding will always want something in return. And all too often that seemingly innocent process of barter will turn out to be far from benign.

On the other hand, I do believe that we can practice certain techniques that may help us to create the proper attitude of acceptance that may encourage the participation of a spirit teacher in our life and may bring about a clearer vision of our path on our Earthwalk. I also believe that the disciplined practice of certain meditation or visualization exercises may enable us to "hear" more clearly the soft whispers of angelic guidance and to perceive more completely the full meaning of the heavenly messages that are sent to us.

I would very strongly urge you to experiment with the following techniques with an attitude of respectfulness to the sacredness that is inherent in the act of communication with your spirit teacher or spirit guide. And you should definitely not practice these exercises with the goal of hoping to see your guide manifest physically in your presence.

Truly, the best attitude to assume is that you are going to enter a state of relaxation and tranquillity whereby higher levels of awareness—perhaps from your *own* individual higher self—will present themselves to you in a manner whereby you might get in deeper touch with important aspects of yourself.

Exercise One: Using the Image of Your Spirit Guide to Experience Unconditional Love, Wisdom, and Higher Awareness: Here is a relaxation technique and exercise that I have employed with great success in numerous seminars and workshops throughout the United States and overseas. If followed correctly, it can place you in a state of consciousness that will enable you to reach out and establish a spiritual linkup with a more aware aspect of yourself and that may prompt your increased perception of contact between you and a spirit guide or teacher.

It is possible for you to read this relaxation technique, pausing now and then to permit its effectiveness to permeate your mental and spiritual essence. If you wish, you may read these techniques aloud, stopping occasionally to contemplate the significance of your inner journey and to receive elevation to a higher state of consciousness.

I would recommend some soft, ethereal background music, classical or New Age, to help you to fashion a mood of tranquillity. Just be certain that the music you choose has no lyrics to distract you.

It may be very helpful to have a trusted friend or family member read these instructions to you. You may also wish to record your own voice reading this exercise and the one that follows into a cassette and then play the tape back, allowing your own voice to guide you.

Any of these methods can be effective. Your success will depend upon your willingness to permit such an experience to manifest itself in your individual spiritual essence.

THE TEXT

Imagine that you are lying on a blanket on a beautiful stretch of beach. You are lying in the sun or in the shade—whichever you prefer.

You are listening to the sounds of Mother Ocean, listening to the rhythmic sounds of the waves as they lap against the shore. You are listening to the same soothing, restful lullaby that Mother Ocean has been singing to men and to women for thousands and thousands of years.

As you relax, you know that nothing will disturb you, nothing will distress you, nothing will molest you or bother you in any way.

Even now you are becoming aware of a golden light of love, wisdom, and knowledge that is moving over you and protecting you from all negativity.

You know that this golden light of love from the God Force of the Universe protects you from all evil and negativity.

You have nothing to fear. Nothing can harm you on any level—body, mind, or spirit.

As you listen to the sound of the ocean waves, you feel all tension leaving your body. The very sound of the waves helps you to become more and more relaxed.

With every breath you take, you find yourself feeling better, more positive in body, mind, and spirit. With every breath that you take, you find yourself becoming more and more relaxed, relaxed.

You know that your body must relax so the real you may rise higher and higher to greater states of awareness.

And now you are feeling a beautiful, soothing energy of

tranquillity, peace, and love entering your feet, and you feel every muscle in your feet relaxing.

That beautiful, soothing energy of tranquillity, peace, and love moves up your legs, into your ankles, your calves, your knees, your thighs, and you feel every muscle in your ankles, your calves, your knees, your thighs relaxing, relaxing, relaxing.

If you should hear any sound at all other than the sound of my voice, you will relax even more. If you should hear any sound at all—a slamming door, a honking horn, a shouting voice—that sound will not disturb you in any way. That sound will only help you to relax even more.

Nothing will disturb you. Nothing will distress you in any way.

And now that beautiful energy of tranquillity, peace, and love is moving up to your hips, your stomach, your back, and you feel every muscle in your hips, your stomach, your back relaxing, relaxing, relaxing.

With every breath that you take, you find that your body is becoming more and more relaxed.

And now the beautiful energy of tranquillity, peace, and love enters your chest, your shoulders, your arms, your palms, your fingers, and you feel every muscle in your chest, your shoulders, your arms, your palms, and your fingers relaxing, relaxing, relaxing.

With every breath you take, you find that you are becoming more and more relaxed. Every part of your body is becoming free of tension.

And now that beautiful energy of tranquillity, peace, and love moves into your neck, your face, the very top of your head, and you feel every muscle in your neck, your face, and the very top of your head relaxing, relaxing, relaxing, relaxing.

Your body is now relaxing, but your inner self, your true self, is very much aware.

And now a beautiful golden light is moving all around you. You are not afraid. You feel only love. You know that the golden light signals the presence of your guide, your guardian spirit.

Feel the love as this presence moves over you. Feel the vibrations of love moving over you—warm, peaceful, tranquil.

You know that within the essence of this golden light is a spirit being who has always loved you just as you are.

You have been aware of this loving, guiding presence ever since you were a child, a very small child.

You have been aware that this spiritual intelligence has always loved you just as you are—no facades, no masks, no pretenses.

This spiritual presence loves you unconditionally. This spiritual being loves you with Heavenly love, love that accepts you just as you are.

You feel unconditional love moving all around you. Feel the love that flows to you from your angel guide to you.

And now *look*! Two eyes are beginning to form in the midst of the golden light. You are beholding the eyes of your spirit guide. Feel the love flowing to you from your spirit guide.

Now a face is forming. Oh, look at the smile on the lips of your angelic guide. Feel the love that flows from your guide to your inner being.

Now a body is forming. Behold the beauty of form, structure, and stature of your spiritual guide. *Feel* the love that flows to you from the very presence of your angelic guide.

Your guide is now stretching forth a loving hand to you. Take that hand in yours. Feel that spirit hand in your own. Feel the love flowing through you. Feel the love as your spiritual essence blends with that of your angel guide.

Now, hand in hand, you feel yourself being lifted higher

and higher. Your guide is taking you to a higher dimension of
awareness and love. You are moving higher, higher, higher.

Colors and lights are moving around you ... red, orange,
yellow, green, blue, violet, purple, gold.

Stars seem to be moving around you. It seems as though
you are moving through the universe.

It seems as though you are moving into another dimension
of time and space.

You are moving into a higher vibration of reality.

You are moving to a higher level of awareness, a higher
level of consciousness.

You are becoming aware of a beautiful, spiritual place—
your true home beyond the stars.

Understand that you have within you the ability to rise to
higher levels of awareness and to make contact with higher
aspects of your inner being and the love of your spirit guide.

Understand that you never walk alone, that you are never
friendless, that you are never unloved.

Understand that you have the ability to travel with your
spirit guide to a higher level of awareness where you can experience love as you have never felt it on Earth. Love as you
have yearned for all of your life.

Feel that love now; feel it all around you.

[Pause for two or three minutes to experience this beautiful,
tranquil unconditional love from the spirit guide and a higher
level of awareness.]

And now you are returning from this beautiful, tranquil
state of love and relaxation feeling better than you have felt in
weeks and weeks, months and months.

At the count of five, you will be fully awake and filled with
the wonderful feelings of love, wisdom, and knowledge from
your spirit guide.

One, coming awake. *Two,* coming more and more awake,
filled with love. *Three,* coming more and more awake, filled

with unconditional love from your spirit guide. *Four,* coming awake, opening and closing your hands. *Five,* wide awake and feeling wonderful.

Exercise Two: Using the Image of the Spirit Teacher as a Problem-solving Device: Use the same relaxation technique you employed in Exercise One to place yourself in a state of receptivity for the following problem-solving device. Read the step-by-step process of complete body relaxation so that the Real You is fully prepared to meet the image of your spirit teacher. Although the masculine pronoun is used in this example, you may of course use the feminine pronoun if you wish to do so.

THE TEXT

See yourself walking up a narrow mountain trail in the light of a full moon. The trail is easy to see in the moonlight, and you have no fear of falling.

You are approaching an ashram, a place of spiritual retreat, wherein resides a very ancient and wise spirit teacher.

Take a moment now to experience fully your emotions as you walk up the mountain trail to meet the spirit teacher.

Feel deeply. Savor your expectations.

The spirit teacher whom you are seeking is said to be able to answer any questions sincerely put to him. You are pleased that you have received an invitation from this ancient teacher to visit his ashram in this dimension of time and space and to ask him any question that troubles you.

Now you turn off the mountain trail and begin to walk up the path that leads to the front gate of the ashram. Be aware of your inner thoughts and feelings.

As you enter the gate, you are able to see the dancing flames of a great open fire burning in the center of a courtyard. You are able to see a man dressed in robes sitting near the fire. You know that it is the ancient and wise spirit teacher.

Become totally aware of the spirit teacher.

See his clothes, his body form, his face, his eyes, his mouth, the way he holds and moves his hands.

He gestures to you that you should be seated, and he hands you a cup of his favorite tea.

Raise the cup to your lips. Taste the tea in your mouth. It is a very special tea, exceedingly flavorful, yet mild, gentle to your palate.

The spirit teacher nods to you, indicating that you may now ask a question that is important to you—one that is troubling you.

As you ask your question, notice how the spirit teacher responds to your words. See how carefully he listens. See how thoughtfully he considers your question.

Observe the spirit teacher closely.

He may answer your question with a facial expression alone.

He may choose to answer your question with a gesture of the hands or a shrug of the shoulders.

Or he may answer your question at some length with carefully selected words.

He may show you something. Some object or symbol may appear in his hands.

However he responds, he is answering you *now*!

[Pause here for about two minutes to allow the impressions to come.]

What kind of reply did he give you?

What answer did you receive?

How do you feel about his answer? Are you pleased or displeased?

How do you feel toward the spirit teacher?

The spirit teacher tells you that it is now time to return to your dimension of time and space.

Before you leave, he reaches into his robe and brings forth a leather pouch. He tells you that he has a very special gift to present to you. He wishes you to take the object with you.

He opens the leather bag and removes your gift. Look at it. See what it is.

Tell the spirit teacher how you feel about him and his gift. Say good-bye, for now you must leave.

As you walk down the path to the mountain trail, open your hands and look at your gift once again in the moonlight. Turn it over in your hands. Feel it. Discover all you can about the gift.

What deep significance does this gift have for you?

Understand that you have the ability to use this gift wisely and to its most positive advantage.

Now begin walking down the mountain trail, carrying your gift with you.

And now, with the thoughts of the spirit teacher forever in your memory, with the true meaning and value of his gift forever impressed in your awareness, begin to return to full consciousness.

[Count down to five as in Exercise One.]

Dr. S. Ralph Harlow has given an account of the angelic experience that he shared with his wife, Marion, on a lovely spring morning while walking in the woods near Ballardvale, Massachusetts, circa 1933. At first they heard only the sound of muted voices. Then, looking upward about ten feet, they beheld "a floating group of glorious, beautiful creatures that glowed with spiritual beauty."

Dr. Harlow, who had earned degrees from Harvard, Columbia, and the Hartford Theological Seminary, said that the group of entities was composed of six beautiful young women dressed in flowing white garments, apparently engaged in earnest conversation. Neither he nor his wife could understand complete words or phrases, although their voices were clearly audible.

"If they were aware of our existence they gave no indication of it," Dr. Harlow wrote in the December 1986 issue of *Guideposts* magazine. "Their faces were perfectly clear to us, and one woman, slightly older than the rest, was especially beautiful. . . . She was talking intently to a younger spirit whose back was toward us and who looked up into the face of the woman who was talking."

Stating firmly the truthfulness and accuracy of his account, Dr. Harlow said that the experience made both him and his wife more "aware of the host of heaven all about us," and he testified that their lives had been filled with a "wonderful hope."

Even as a theologian with his doctorate, Dr. Harlow admitted that he had often been puzzled by the assertion of St. Paul that we have bodies other than those of our normal flesh and blood. But since he and his wife had seen the angels, Dr. Harlow felt that he could comprehend more fully the words of St. Paul in I Corinthians 15:40-49: "There are also celestial bodies, and bodies terrestrial: but the glory of the celestial is one, and the glory of the terrestrial is another. . . . So also is the resurrection of the dead. . . . It is sown a natural body; it is raised a spiritual body. There is a natural body and a spiritual body. . . . And as we have borne the image of the earthly, we shall also bear the image of the heavenly."

I have come to understand that our cosmic companions—be they spirits of the deceased who maintain a loving interest toward us or a created company of entities that came into existence sometime before the Earth was fashioned— have, as a considerable portion of their mission, the task of guiding us toward ever-expanding mental and spiritual aware- ness. As well as their having been assigned to be there on oc- casion to give us a helping hand, I believe that it is also an integral part of their terrestrial task to lead us to a clearer understanding of our true role in the universal scheme of things.

And it seems to be very clear to me, judging from my own interaction with the cowled teacher, that while these beings very often cast themselves in the roles of our tutors, they favor teaching us by example and inspiration rather than by direct intervention in our learning process.

It is in this crucial area of noninterference that the good spirits and angelic beings differ markedly from the entities that emanate from the Dark Side. The less benign beings have no compunction about interfering with humankind's spiritual evolution. On the contrary, they appear to delight in a pro- grammed manipulation of our spiritual destiny, the exploita- tion of our physical bodies, and the enslavement of our souls.

Throughout our human history the benevolent beings have shown us by their examples that the impossible can be ac- complished, that the rules of our physics are made to be bro- ken, and that the physical laws of this planet were created to serve, rather than subvert, the human spirit.

My own research and insights have made me certain that these benign spiritual helpers have absolutely no interest in living our lives for us or in permanently delivering us from temptation, trials, or torments. While they may on occasion be there to guide or inspire us to achieve a greater understanding of the true reality of things—and while they may on even rarer occasions actually intervene in certain physical mishaps during our Earthwalk—their essential message is that we must learn how to manage our own affairs, discover how to achieve balance in our own lives, and strive to accomplish our own deliverance from the dangers and hazards inherent in our planetary existence on Earth.

If readers should wish to participate in Brad Steiger's continuing research into the mystery of Guardian Angels and Spirit Guides, they may obtain a copy of the Steiger Questionnaire of Mystical, Paranormal, and UFO experiences by sending a stamped, self-addressed envelope (#10 business-sized) to:

Brad Steiger
P.O. Box 434
Forest City, IA 50436